FRENCH BUSINESS CORRESPONDENCE COURSE

9.25

FRENCH BUSINESS CORRESPONDENCE COURSE

Derrik Ferney
B.A., M.A., M.Sc., P.G.C.E.

School of Languages and European Studies
The Polytechnic, Wolverhampton

MACMILLAN MULTILINGUAL BUSINESS SERIES

MACMILLAN

First published in 1989 by
THE MACMILLAN PRESS LTD
Houndmills, Basingstoke, Hampshire RG21 2XS
and London
Companies and representatives throughout the world

ISBN 0–333–49433–4

Typeset by Gecko Limited, Bicester, Oxon

Printed in Malaysia

A catalogue record for this book is available
from the British Library.

10   9   8   7   6   5   4
00   99   98   97   96   95   94

CONTENTS

ACKNOWLEDGEMENTS

The Author and the Publishers are grateful to Renée Kendall-Tobias and Stuart Williams for the contribution they made to developing the letters in this book. The Author would also like to thank SEGI Services (Gravure-Imprimerie) of Grenoble for the many examples of letter-heads which were made available to him.

ABOUT THIS COURSE

The principle on which the *Multilingual Business Correspondence Course* is based is a simple one. Analysis of any significant corpus of business correspondence reveals that a number of relatively unchanging, context-independent linguistic formulae, in conjunction with a number of context-dependent terms and expressions, account for a significant proportion of the content of business letters.

These formulae, terms and expressions can be regarded as the building blocks of written communications between firms. Letter-writing in the foreign language becomes a considerably easier task if students have access to these building blocks and, through regular practice, are able to assimilate them into their active vocabulary.

The *Multilingual Business Handbook*, with which this Course is intended to be used, gives students easy access to some 1800 of these building blocks in each of 5 languages.

The *Multilingual Business Correspondence Course*, of which this French Course is a part, provides students with the practice required to assimilate them.

This is not of course to say that a knowledge of fixed formulae, terms and expressions is in itself sufficient to account for the creativity inherent in writing business letters in a foreign language, merely that it can provide a useful starting point. The terms and expressions which are contained in the *Multilingual Business Handbook* and used in this Course are no substitute for competence in the foreign language, but they can both help students develop that competence and provide accomplished linguists with access to the business language with which they may be unfamiliar.

INTRODUCTION

This course is intended for Intermediate or Advanced level students of foreign languages for business purposes. In designing the course two major considerations have been borne in mind: that it should be a teaching course and that it should be compatible with modern approaches to language teaching.

A Teaching Course

Regrettably, students often come to perceive letter-writing in the foreign language as an arduous dictionary-based task reminiscent of unseen prose translation. This Course sets out to counter that perception by creating a graded, supportive and realistic learning environment which helps students acquire the translation and composition skills required to deal with business correspondence. This is achieved in the following way:

- Letters are graded in order of increasing linguistic and situational difficulty. Students learn how to compose complex business letters by first dealing with simpler ones.

- The teaching/learning process is supported at every stage by the *Multilingual Business Handbook*. Most of the letters are accompanied by a translation aid in the form of a 'skeleton' of key letters and numbers (A1, B7, R77 etc.) which act as pointers to terms and expressions contained in the *Multilingual Business Handbook*. The provision of 'skeletons' dispenses with the need for lengthy dictionary searches and permits students to deal with complex correspondence relatively quickly.

- Every section contains two scenarios of three letters each. These letters simulate a continuing exchange about a specific issue, for example a disputed insurance claim or damage to goods in transit. The realism implicit in this simulation means that in the classroom, as in real business practice, one can frequently derive key terms, expressions and structures from previous exchanges within the same context, and use them to aid the production of the new letter. This Course is designed to model the association of incoming with outgoing correspondence and to do so in exchanges of increasing linguistic and situational difficulty.

Modern Approaches to Language Teaching

Modern approaches to teaching languages for business purposes tend to assess student learning by means of integrated exercises or assignments. These consist of simulations of business activities involving case studies, role playing and the deployment of a range of listening, speaking, reading and writing skills to accomplish a set of realistic tasks. The translating and writing of business letters normally feature quite prominently in the assignment-based approach, not only because of the realism inherent in such tasks but also because they act as an appropriate vehicle for practising writing in the foreign language. This Course aims precisely to provide, within the context of the assignment-based approach, the regularity of practice and the gradual development of skills necessary for successful letter writing in the foreign language.

Modern approaches to learning business languages also tend to stress the importance of autonomous learning, information retrieval and the use of appropriate materials and technologies to support these activities. This course is uniquely placed in this respect, since it is intended to be used with the *Multilingual Business Handbook*.

This is a definitive guide to commercial letter writing in English, French, German, Spanish and Italian and is currently published in Britain, France, Germany, Italy, Holland, Spain and the United States. It contains approximately 1800 expressions and phrases in each language, divided into sections such as Enquiries and Offers, Orders, etc. Within each section, every expression has a key letter and number (A36, B39 etc.) which corresponds exactly to the appropriate expression in each of the other languages.

Most of the letters in the *Multilingual Business Correspondence Course* are accompanied by a 'skeleton' of the form (A1, A7, B26, C90 etc.) which enables the student to retrieve from the Handbook key phrases which will be of help in the translation of the associated letter.

An Integrated Package

In combination with the *Multilingual Business Handbook* and the *LinguaWrite Computer Database*, the *Multilingual Business Correspondence Course* provides an integrated and pedagogically sound learning package which is compatible with modern language teaching practice. It can be used on a stand-alone basis or as a complement to the assignment-based approach to enable students to learn about business correspondence by translating and writing letters of increasing complexity. Furthermore the database provides students with the opportunity of using information technology as an integral part of the learning process, and can be used with the computer's word-processing facility to enable letters of business quality to be produced.

HOW TO USE THIS COURSE

The Course Structure

The course is divided into 15 sections, each of which is based on one or more sections of the *Multilingual Business Handbook*. The sections are further divided into two sub-sections, A and B, with three letters in each. Each letter is identified according to the sub-section and section to which it belongs. For example, Section 1 of the course contains letters 1A1, 1A2, 1A3, 1B1, 1B2 and 1B3. Section 2 contains letters 2A1, 2A2, 2A3, 2B1, 2B2 and 2B3, etc.

Different Paths through the Course

Those letters whose identifier contains the character A are primarily intended for use by students who have already completed a course of study in French, and who are continuing with the language in preparation for A/S level or the intermediate awards of bodies such as BTEC, RSA, Institute of Linguists or LCCI. Those letters whose identifier contains the character B are primarily intended for use by higher diploma or degree level students of French for business purposes, including those preparing for higher level RSA or Institute of Linguists examinations. The Course thus provides for different start-levels according to the students' prior experience of the language.

Teachers wishing to provide a course aimed primarily at post-GCSE (or equivalent) students can work on the simpler sub-section A of each section, whilst post 'A' Level (or equivalent) students can work on the corresponding but more complex sub-section B. Conversely teachers may decide to ignore this distinction and simply work through the course section by section, selecting letters from both sub-sections as they see fit.

Different paths can thus be followed through the course according to student needs.

Section Layout

Each section of the Course deals with a different type of letter and is divided into two sub-sections comprising three letters each. The three letters are associated by situation and context, simulating ongoing correspondence between foreign and British companies. Letter 1 of each sub-section is written in the foreign language for translation into the student's mother tongue. A 'skeleton' of key letters and numbers taken from the *Multilingual Business Handbook* points the student towards the key phrases contained in the letter and acts as a translation aid. Each sub-section has been devised so that many of the terms and expressions learned by the student in the course of translating letter 1 into his/her mother tongue can subsequently be used to translate letter 2 into the target language.
Again a 'skeleton' is provided for this translation task. Letter 3 then provides the opportunity for further practice, continuing the exchange commenced by letters 1 and 2 but allowing the student freer expression, not only because of its guided composition format, but also because it is not accompanied by a 'skeleton' derived from the *Handbook*. Typically, then, the teacher might work with students on letters 1 and 2 in class and set the associated letter 3 as a homework exercise.

Progress through the Sections

The letters contained in the sections increase in complexity as students progress through the Course. This increase in complexity manifests itself in a number of ways. Firstly, the situations dealt with in the sections become progressively more elaborate, with a concomitant increase in letter length. Secondly, the language structures and terminology used increase in difficulty and specificity, and the role of tone is developed. Thirdly, the proportion of a given letter accounted for by the terms and expressions whose key letters and numbers are found in the associated skeleton diminishes as the Course proceeds. This is particularly true of the later letters in the foreign language, which are designed to expose students to a variety of terms, expressions and language structures not contained in the *Multilingual Business Handbook*. These are then reworked in the reply, the composition of which is aided by the usual skeleton of key letters and numbers, which point students to helpful terms and expressions in the *Multilingual Business Handbook*. Here again, in the later sections students will be expected to modify these terms and expressions to suit specific situations of use. The need to effect tense shifts, change syntax and substitute vocabulary means that students gradually come to use the building blocks as a springboard for creative writing in the foreign language.

Letter Layout

Letter layout is a moot point. Various sets of 'rules' have been suggested, but in reality the practices adopted by firms often defy these supposed conventions. For example, some firms clearly regard letter-heads and letter layout as important and distinctive features of house style, and consciously choose to break with what they regard as conventional layout. Extrinsic factors such as the type of envelope a firm normally uses can also influence letter layout, with window envelopes, for example, usually requiring the recipient's address to be positioned adjacent to the left-hand margin of the letter in Britain and the right-hand margin of the letter in France. The various letter layouts used in this Course reflect current business practice and are intended to cover the most important aspects of format in as clear a manner as possible. They should not, however, be regarded as prescriptive and students will, in any case, quickly discover the particular practices of their employer upon starting work or commencing a training period.

Students preparing for public examinations in which letter layout is a component should of course follow the rules for layout prescribed by the Examination Board in question.

SUMMARY OF COURSE AIMS

The *Multilingual Business Correspondence Course* aims to provide:

1. A structured teaching/learning package as opposed to a corpus of business correspondence.
2. Materials which can be equally well used on a stand-alone basis or as part of an assignment-based course.
3. Maximum opportunity for autonomous learning on the part of the student, through its integration with the *Multilingual Business Handbook*.
4. The opportunity for students to use information technology as a regular part of their learning activities, through its integration with the *LinguaWrite Computer Database*.
5. Different paths through the course for students of different language levels.
6. A realistic learning environment in which business letters are associated by function and context in a genuinely communicative manner.
7. A pedagogically sound learning environment in which letter reception precedes letter production.
8. An enjoyable learning experience for students, by focusing on what they can do as opposed to what they cannot.

SECTION 1:   ENQUIRIES AND OFFERS

This section is based on terms and expressions contained in Section B of the *MULTILINGUAL BUSINESS HANDBOOK*.

FRANCE – EUROPE
27 rue de la Chapelle
75011 PARIS

Tél: (1) 34.33.22.44

Universal Office Supplies
356 Hagley Road
BIRMINGHAM
Angleterre

N/Réf: JF/BC 150
Objet: Demande de renseignements

Paris, le 2 novembre 19

Messieurs,

A la suite de notre conversation téléphonique du 30 octobre dernier, nous vous prions de nous envoyer votre dernier catalogue concernant les machines de traitement de texte et l'équipement de bureau le plus récent.

we'd be grateful

Nous vous saurions gré également de nous faire parvenir des renseignements sur vos prix, *particulars* conditions de vente et délais de livraison. *timescales*

Dans l'attente d'une prompte réponse, nous vous prions d'agréer, Messieurs, nos salutations distinguées.

J. FABRE
Directeur des Achats

(*Multilingual Business Handbook skeleton:* A14, A8, A2, A18, B11, A45, B94, A123, A128)

Universal Office Supplies
356 Hagley Road
BIRMINGHAM

Tel: (0)21 446 7432
Fax: (0)21 300 3100

12 November 19

Your Reference: JF/BC 150
Our Reference: HA/JF 112

Monsieur J. Fabre
Directeur des Achats
France – Europe
27 rue de la Chapelle
75011 Paris
France

Dear Sir

We thank you for your letter of the 2nd of this month. Please find enclosed our catalogue of word-processing machines and other office equipment.

Our prices are quoted in the enclosed list. They are CIF and we can offer an export rebate of 5% for payment within one month of dispatch. This offer is firm subject to acceptance by 15 December.

We thank you for your enquiry about our goods and hope we have been of help to you.

Yours faithfully

Herbert Atkins
Manager

(*Multilingual Business Handbook skeleton:* A13, A14, A1, A10, A11, A34, B76, B110, B96, B120, B123, A124)

Continue the preceding exchange of correspondence by composing a third letter (in French) on the basis of the following notes.

To: Herbert Atkins (Universal Office Supplies)

From: J. Fabre (France-Europe)

- Further to our enquiry (date) and your reply (date), thank you for the information.

- Is there any discount for quantity (e.g. ten machines)?

- Can we be assured that the software of the BECSTAR wordprocessor has all the characters needed for French, German and Spanish?

- The range of office equipment you offer does not include Facsimile machines. Can you supply these?

- Thank you in advance for this supplementary information.

Yours etc.

Agro-Machines S.A.
111 Boulevard du Général de Gaulle
03012 Moulins

Tél: 70.44.13.26

Perkins Farming Supplies
46 Rathbone Road
Aylesbury
Buckinghamshire
Angleterre

N/Réf: JMB/AB 1032

Moulins, le 27 septembre 19

A l'attention de Monsieur G. Jones

Monsieur,

A la suite de notre réunion à l'exposition de Lyon, nous vous saurions gré de nous faire parvenir par retour de courrier des renseignements au sujet de vos machines agricoles.

Nous aimerions offrir à nos clients une gamme plus étendue de machines et nous savons que les semoirs et herses intéresseraient particulièrement certains d'entre eux. C'est pourquoi nous serions prêts à vous passer une commande d'essai à condition que la qualité et les prix de vos articles soient satisfaisants.

Veuillez nous indiquer vos prix de gros et nous faire savoir si vous pouvez nous accorder une remise. Nous aimerions également connaître vos conditions de paiement.

Dans l'attente d'une prompte réponse, nous vous prions d'agréer, Monsieur, l'expression de nos sentiments distingués.

J-M Bévillard
Directeur Commercial

(*Multilingual Business Handbook skeleton:* A14, A6, A1, A29, A45, A53, B125, B65, B74, B82, B84, A123, A128)

Perkins Farming Supplies
46 Rathbone Road
AYLESBURY
Buckinghamshire

Tel: (0)296 614832

Fax: (0)296 614800

Your Ref: JMB/AB 1032
Our Ref: GJ/BC 172

2 October 19

For the attention of Mr J-M Bévillard

Agro-Machines S.A.
111 Boulevard du Général de Gaulle
F 03012 Moulins
France

Dear Sir

We thank you for your letter of 27 September. Please find enclosed our catalogue with details of prices, delivery times and terms of payment. We should like to draw your special attention to our introductory discount of 2%.

You will find the details of seed drills and harrows on pages 30 and 72 of the catalogue. All our products carry a 2-year guarantee and we replace defective parts free of charge.

We are able to assure you that your orders will be executed promptly and with great care.

We await your further instructions.

Yours faithfully

Geoffrey Jones

Manager PFS

(*Multilingual Business Handbook skeleton:* A13, A14, A6, A1, A10, A34, B94, B84, B27, B81, B39, B40, B133, C60)

Continue the preceding exchange of correspondence by composing a third letter (in French) on the basis of the following notes.

To: Geoffrey Jones (Perkins Farming Supplies)

From: J-M Bévillard (Agro-Machines S.A.)

Subject: Your catalogue

- Thank you for your reply (date) to our enquiry (date).

- Can you offer a discount greater than 2% if the value of the order exceeds £500?

- How long would it take to send a replacement part to France in case of breakdown?

- We are very interested by many items in your catalogue and would like to send a colleague to visit you in the New Year. Alternatively, we would be pleased to receive a visit from one of your colleagues.

- In the meantime can you let us have more information about the excavator on p. 103.

SECTION 2: ORDERS

This section is based on terms and expressions contained in Section C of the *MULTILINGUAL BUSINESS HANDBOOK*.

DRAPERIE DU SENTIER

Tél: (1) 43.64.75.99

25 rue du Sentier
75002 PARIS

Northern Textiles
115 Manchester Road
SALFORD
Angleterre

N/Réf: 329 CB 87

Paris, le 18 novembre 19

Messieurs,

further to

A la suite de notre conversation téléphonique d'hier nous vous prions de trouver ci-joint notre bon de commande no 329. *order (form)*

carriage paid. items wd. past-stress is requested esp. sheets

Veuillez nous envoyer immédiatement les articles mentionnés (taies d'oreiller, draps et couvre-lits) en port payé à domicile. Nous insistons particulièrement sur l'importance que nous attachons au délai de livraison étant donné la proximité des fêtes de fin d'année.

of delivery times in view of the approach of the Xmas period. bedside mats.

Pourriez-vous en même temps nous envoyer des échantillons de descentes de lit et de housses de couette? Nous sommes engagés vis-à-vis d'un autre fournisseur mais la qualité de ses produits laisse à désirer. *committed to another*

is unsatisfactory above

Veuillez confirmer la commande mentionnée ci-dessus aussitôt que possible et agréer, Messieurs, nos salutations distinguées.

C. Béranger
Chef des Ventes

(*Multilingual Business Handbook skeleton*: A18, C11, C12, B105, C14/15, C2, C23, C63, A127)

Northern Textiles
115 Manchester Road
SALFORD

Tel: 061 442 3672

Your Reference: 329 CB 87
Our Reference: 476 FJ

27 November 19

For the attention of Mr C Béranger

Draperie du Sentier
25 rue du Sentier
75002 PARIS
France

Dear Sir

entretenir

Thank you for your letter of the 18th inst. We are pleased to enter into business relations with you.

We confirm your order and will execute it as soon as possible. Unfortunately, however, we must modify it slightly; because of a shortage of raw materials, we cannot supply all the bedspreads that you require at the moment. We shall therefore send the goods in two consignments and hope that this modification is acceptable to you.

We are also sending you samples of bedside mats and duvet covers as you request.

We hope that the quality of the goods will meet your expectations and we await your further instructions.

Yours faithfully

Fred Jarvis
Export Sales Manager

Enclosures: Samples

(*Multilingual Business Handbook skeleton:* A13, A14, A6, A1, A10, A11, A32, A76, C56, C57, C30, C35, C32, D35, C31, B48, B124, C60, A129)

Continue the preceding exchange of correspondence by composing a third letter (in French) on the basis of the following notes.

To: C. Béranger (Draperie du Sentier)

From: Fred Jarvis (Northern Textiles)

- Further to our letter of 27 November we are now able to deliver the rest of the bedspreads you ordered.

- They are being dispatched today.

- We are sending you more samples of duvet covers.

- Also a copy of our latest catalogue.

- We refer you to pp. 134-143, our range of bedroom accessories.

- One of our partners will be in Paris in late January. Will it be convenient for him to call?

LE JOUET POITEVIN
Route de Niort
B.P. 123 X
86038 POITIERS CEDEX

Tél: 49.88.02.88

Playshop
14 Fieldhouse Fold
SHEFFIELD
Yorkshire
Angleterre

Poitiers, le 7 mars 19

A l'attention de Mr F. Baker

Monsieur,

Nous vous remercions de votre lettre du 2 courant ainsi que de votre catalogue et des échantillons.

Nous avons soigneusement examiné ces derniers et nous désirons commander 5 exemplaires de chacun des articles suivants: jeux de construction A14, assortiments de briques A32, modèles réduits de garage D73 et modèles réduits d'aéroport D75. Les fêtes de Pâques étant très proches, nous aurions besoin de ces articles d'ici 3 semaines et nous aimerions que vous nous fassiez savoir par télex quand cette livraison pourrait être effectuée.

Nous avons remarqué que vos prix comprennent l'assurance et le port payé jusqu'à Paris et que vous accordez une remise de 10% sur les prix catalogue, ce dont nous vous remercions.

Nous vous serions reconnaissants d'exécuter cette commande aussi promptement et soigneusement que possible. Nous avons l'intention de vous passer des commandes plus importantes si ces marchandises nous donnent entière satisfaction.

Nous vous prions d'agréer, Monsieur, nos meilleures salutations.

G. Dutilleul
Directeur des Achats

(*Multilingual Business Handbook skeleton*: A6, A1, A10, A11, C2, C10, C14, D8, B97, B105, B80, B133, B127, B126)

Playshop
14 Fieldhouse Fold
SHEFFIELD
Yorkshire

Tel: (0)742 621435
Telex: PLASHEF 420721
Fax: 0742 900 010

15 March 19

For the attention of Mr Gérard Dutilleul

Le Jouet Poitevin
Route de Niort
B.P. 123 X
86038 POITIERS CEDEX
France

Dear Sir

We acknowledge receipt of your letter of the 7th of this month. However we regret to inform you that it will not be possible to deliver the goods within the 3 week period that you specify.

nous trouvons dans l'impossibilité de *preciser*

Because of a strike affecting some of our employees we are behind with production. Whilst we will be able to send you all the model garages and airports, as these can be supplied from stock, we will unfortunately be unable to start manufacture of the other articles in your order until the middle of April.

We hope that this modification is acceptable to you and await your further instructions before sending part of your order and starting manufacture of the other part. As soon as we receive instructions we shall send you our advice of despatch.

We deeply regret this change to your order.

Yours faithfully

Frederick Baker
Chief Buyer

(*Multilingual Business Handbook skeleton:* A6, A9, A11, A32, D24, C34, C37, C13, C50, C31, C62, D43, A43, C31)

Continue the preceding exchange of correspondence by composing a third letter (in French) on the basis of the following notes.

To: F. Baker (Playshop)

From: G. Dutilleul (Le Jouet Poitevin)

- Thank you for your letter of 15 March.

- Sorry about the strike and its effect on your production.

- Unfortunately we must cancel that part of the order that you cannot fulfil.

- We are sure that you will understand that we must have the goods sooner rather than later.

- We will therefore have to go to another supplier for some of the articles.

- We have no doubt that we will be placing larger orders with you in the future.

SECTION 3:   DELIVERY, TRANSPORT, CUSTOMS

This section is based on terms and expressions contained in Section D of the *MULTILINGUAL BUSINESS HANDBOOK*.

Les Caves de Bourgogne

15 rue Jean Jaurès
21200 Beaune

Tel: 80 22 22 71

Arrow Wine Importers
5 Salop Street
Wolverhampton
WV1 1LV
Angleterre

Beaune, le 28 novembre 19

Objet: Votre commande no 467

A l'attention de Mr C. Forrester

Monsieur,

[handwritten: recent letter]

[handwritten: Burgundy] A la suite de votre dernière correspondance concernant votre commande de douze caisses de vin de Bourgogne, Juliénas 1976, nous sommes heureux de vous faire savoir que nous pouvons vous livrer ces marchandises immédiatement. Etant donné que vous ne précisez pas le moyen de transport que vous désirez, nous avons décidé de vous envoyer ces marchandises par camion, selon nos habitudes, en une seule expédition. *[handwritten: delivery/consignment]*

[handwritten: Given that your order does not state how the goods are to be transported]

[handwritten: single]

Bien qu'il s'agisse d'articles fragiles, nous pouvons vous assurer qu'ils vous parviendront en bon état car nos emballages sont à l'épreuve de tout dégât. *[handwritten: guarantee · reach you in gd. cond. · packaging capable of withstands · any kind of damage / damage-proof]*

[handwritten: despatch dves.] Veuillez trouver ci-joint les documents d'expédition dont vous aurez besoin. Nous devons en effet vous informer que vous devrez payer les droits d'entrée sur les marchandises importées. *[handwritten: require · Must/sho · will have to · import duty · goods.]*

Nous espérons que vous accepterez ces conditions et nous serions heureux que vous confirmiez la commande mentionnée ci-dessus aussitôt que possible. *[handwritten: above]*

Veuillez agréer, Monsieur, l'expression de nos sentiments distingués.

B. Montory
Directeur

(*Multilingual Business Handbook skeleton*: D5, D45, D51, D35, D32, D107, D98, D40, D121, C63, A6, A128)

Arrow Wine Importers
5 Salop Street
Wolverhampton
WV1 1LV

Tel: (0)902 53724
Telex: ARR207462

3 December 19

For the attention of Mr B. Montory

Les Caves de Bourgogne
15 rue Jean Jaurès
21200 Beaune
France

Dear Sir

[handwritten: tout de suite / immédiatement]
[handwritten: Nous vous saurions gré / de nous faire]
[handwritten: Nous nous en inquiétons]
[handwritten: Nous n'avons pas encore reçu les march.]
[handwritten: l'envoi]

I am replying at once to your letter of 28th of last month. We have not yet received the *[handwritten: vu/]*
consignment of Juliénas 76 and are becoming anxious because of the proximity of *[handwritten: étant donné la]*
Christmas. Can you let us know the reason for this delay, by telex if possible. *[handwritten: proximité des fêtes]*
[handwritten: Veuillez nous faire connaître les raisons de ce retard par télex] *[handwritten: de fin d'année!]*
[handwritten: désirons vous confier la commande suivante] *[handwritten: six caisses]*

We also wish to place a new order with you for another half dozen cases of Château de
Beaune 82 and a dozen cases of this year's Beaujolais Nouveau. (See your catalogue pp. 102
and 131.) *[handwritten: douze]* *[handwritten: supplémentaires/de plus]*
[handwritten: vous passer] *[handwritten: Nous cherchons une liv. immé / d'urgence]* *[handwritten: (Nous vous référons)]* *[handwritten: Voir votre catalogue]*

Once more we require delivery urgently and we would ask you to send the goods inclusive of
freight and in shockproof cases in order to reduce damage in transit to a minimum. *[handwritten: fret compris]*
[handwritten: à l'épreuve des chocs anti-choc] *[handwritten: réduire au minimum les dommages en]*
[handwritten: résistant aux chocs] *[handwritten: éviter les risques]* *[handwritten: cours de route]*
We understand that we will have to pay import duty on the goods. *[handwritten: devrons]*
[handwritten: en transit/transport]

We hope for an early reply and trust that the first consignment will arrive in the near
future. *[handwritten: Dans l'espoir d'une prompte réponse]* *[handwritten: dans un proche ? avenir]*

Yours faithfully

Charles Forrester
Manager

(Multilingual Business Handbook skeleton: A6, A16, D26, D27, C6, D6, D55, D96, D87, D59, D121, A123, A104)

Continue the preceding exchange of correspondence by composing a third letter (in French) on the basis of the following notes.

To: Charles Forrester (Arrow Wine Importers)

From: Albert Sorel (Les Caves de Bourgogne)

Notre compagnie/société ne possède pas de télex. C'est pourqu[oi] je m'empresse de vous répondre par écr[it]
ne disposons pas de

- We do not have a telex so I am writing as quickly as possible.

est tombé malade fin n.   *à sa place*

*   - Mr Montory became ill at the end of November and I am therefore writing in his place (Albert Sorel).

Nous nous excusons du retard de/(dans)/apporté à l'expédition,   dû à
exprimer nos regrets concernant le retard dans l'envoi

- We regret the delay in dispatching your Juliénas 76, which was due to M. Montory's illness.

expédié   en même temps que   commande

- The wine has now been dispatched together with your second order (Château de Beaune and Beaujolais Nouveau). Our stock of the latter is quickly running out.   *épuise   s'épuis[e]*
Vous pouvez   de celui-ci   ce dernier est en train de   être épuisé   rapidem[ent]
s'épuiser

- You can rely on us to pay careful attention to our packing. We will in any case make good any breakages.
compter sur nous. en ce qui concerne   En tout cas   (compenser)
vous pouvez   prêter toute notre attention   De toute ma[nière]   rembourserons
nous faire   à l'emballage.
confiance/nous faire confier l'emballage soigneux   tous dégâts
vous assurer un emballage fiable

* *dans l'expédition de votre commande de J.76, ce qui est dû à la maladie*

Vous pouvez compter sur Nous pour (l'attention) que nous porterons à nos emballages.

bris — breakages

Entrepôts Dupont
400 Boulevard Maréchal Leclerc
69000 LYON

Tél: 78.37.01.55

J.R. Peters Ltd
Wholesale Food
Supplies
406 Ealing Common
Road London W5
Angleterre

Lyon, le 4 mai 19

A l'attention de M. Peters

Monsieur,

Nous accusons réception de votre lettre du 30 avril et vous en remercions. Nous sommes heureux de confirmer notre commande d'une grosse de fromages de Cheddar de 2 kg. chacun, dont vous trouverez ci-joint le bulletin de commande No. 476.

Comme ces marchandises sont périssables, nous aimerions qu'elles nous soient livrés par camion avant la fin de la quinzaine qui suit, en une seule expédition. Nous vous prions de prêter toute votre attention à l'emballage, vu les conditions climatiques inhabituelles que nous connaissons à l'heure actuelle.

Etant donné les nouveaux règlements douaniers qui doivent entrer prochainement en vigueur, nous aimerions savoir si nous devrons payer des droits d'entrée sur ces marchandises.

Dans l'attente de votre prompte réponse, nous vous prions d'agréer, Monsieur, nos meilleures salutations.

R. Dupont
Directeur Commercial

(*Multilingual Business Handbook skeleton:* A6, A1, A9, A10, C56, C11, D51, D20, D35, D73, D131, D121, A123)

J.R. Peters Ltd
Wholesale Food Supplies
406 Ealing Common Road
London W5

Tel: 01 444 1111

10 May 19

For the attention of Mr René Dupont

Entrepôts Dupont
400 Boulevard Maréchal Leclerc
69000 Lyon
France

Dear Sir

Thank you for your letter of the 4th inst concerning your order of a gross of Cheddar cheeses.

Since we need approximately a fortnight to complete any foreign order, the delivery dates in your letter cannot be exactly adhered to. We must also inform you that in order to reduce damage in transit to a minimum our goods are always carefully packed and are dispatched by refrigerated truck.

Concerning the import duty on these goods, we shall attend to the customs formalities and adjust your invoice accordingly.

As you require delivery urgently we shall execute your order as soon as possible, without awaiting further instructions. We trust these conditions will be acceptable to you.

Yours faithfully

Frederick Peters
General Manager

(*Multilingual Business Handbook skeleton:* A6, A1, A10, C64, D21, D59, D51, D68, D121, D132, E22, D6, C57, C60)

Continue the preceding exchange of correspondence by composing a third letter (in French) on the basis of the following notes.

To: Frederick Peters (J.R. Peters Ltd)

From: René Dupont (Laiteries Dupont)

- Thanks for your letter of the 10th inst.

- We are happy with your conditions and and hope that the order will have been dispatched by the time you receive this letter.

- Thank you also for looking after the import formalities.

- Our accountants will be contacting the relevant government department in France to obtain a clear picture of the current regulations regarding the import of foodstuffs from other member countries of the EEC.

- Please let us know whether one of your colleagues is due to be in our part of the world in the near future.

SECTION 4:   INVOICES, PAYMENTS AND REMINDERS

This section is based on terms and expressions contained in Section E of the *MULTILINGUAL BUSINESS HANDBOOK*.

Garage Leroy
Concessionnaire Aston
Rue Grande
F-77210 AVON

Tél: 33.58.03.88

Aston Rubery Group
Longfield Plant
Longfield Road
OXFORD
Angleterre

Avon, le 26 octobre 19

A l'attention de Mr B. Jones

Monsieur,

Nous sommes heureux de vous faire savoir que votre expédition de pièces de rechange pour Town et GT Mistrals est arrivée hier à notre usine.

Nous sommes obligés de vous signaler qu'il y a une erreur dans votre facture qui ne nous accorde aucun escompte commercial. C'est pourquoi nous vous remettons sous ce pli un eurochèque pour seulement 75% du montant que vous mentionnez. Veuillez nous envoyer un acquit aussitôt que possible ainsi qu'une autre facture rectifiant votre omission.

Nous espérons que vous apprécierez la situation dans laquelle nous nous trouvons. En effet, nous travaillons à marge bénéficiaire réduite et la remise de 5% sur les prix catalogue que vous avez garantie est extrêmement importante.

Nous vous prions d'agréer, Monsieur, nos salutations distinguées.

E. Constant
Directeur Commercial

(Multilingual Business Handbook skeleton: A6, E2, E19, E24, E82, E86, E28, E125, B117, B80)

Nous remettons sous ce pli.

il va de soi que
sans dire
not naturellement

Aston Rubery Group
Longfield Plant
Longfield Road
OXFORD
Tel: (0865) 511 727

3 November 19

For the attention of M. Eric Constant

Garage Leroy
Concessionnaire Aston
Rue Grande
F-77210 AVON
France

Dear Sir

pièces de rechange

We are pleased to note that our consignment of Town and GT Mistral parts arrived in good condition. *en bon état*

votre paiement   *du montant*

We thank you for your payment by eurocheque for three quarters of the amount of the invoice.

une facture rectifiée/modifié

The mistake in our invoice was due to a typing error and an error in our accounts department. Please find enclosed an amended invoice. We will naturally allow you an additional month to pay the debit balance on your account. *accorderons*

régler   solde débiteur de   *proposer/accorder*

We are sorry for the trouble we have caused you; it was always our intention to offer you a discount of 5% on our catalogue prices. *sur les prix catalogue.*

une remise de

Yours faithfully

Nous regrettons le dérangement que nous avons pu vous causer.

vous.
Nous prions de nous
excuser

l'erreur était attribuable à une faute de frappe!
de la part de

Barry Jones   *une erreur dans notre service de comptabilité*
Parts Manager   *à*

Directeur du service des pièces de rechange.
Nous vous accorderons encore un délai deux mois pour
régler votre compte.

(*Multilingual Business Handbook skeleton*: A6, E3, E88, E82, E26, E27, E21, E122, E96, A89, B80)

Continue the preceding exchange of correspondence by composing a third letter (in French) on the basis of the following notes.

To: B. Jones (Aston Rubery Group)

From: E. Constant (Garage Leroy)

la prolongation de

de paiement

- Thank you for the payment extension. *délai supplémentaire ?*

Étant donné la proximité

- Since we are almost at Christmas, we hope January 5th will do. *vous conviendra*

On nous a signalé qu'il existe *fabriqués société.*

- We have heard of a new range of Aston Rubery parts manufactured by a Belgian company Bernhard Joost et Fils.

- Since the Belgians are promising a great deal (quick delivery, top quality) we would like to hear

nb. your opinion. *Vu que / étant donné la compagnie belge nous a fait une* *société* *proposition intéressante*

- We enclose the Joost catalogue for your information.

pour renseignements.

Nous vous remercions de nous avoir accordé une prolongation

• On a attiré notre attention sur
Notre attention a été attiré

qualité haut de gamme
bas de gamme

meilleure qualité
haute qualité

nb. nous aimerions donc savoir ce que
votre société pourrait nous proposer.
de votre côté.

Europ–Export
12 rue Kléber
67012 Strasbourg

Tél: 88 35 12 34

Ashford International
26 Vicarage Road
Small Heath
BIRMINGHAM
Angleterre

Strasbourg, le 3 septembre 19

A l'attention de Mr E. Bennett

Monsieur,

Nous remettons sous ce pli copie de notre facture pour les 10 services de verres en cristal qui vous ont été livrés début juillet. Nous vous avions priés de bien vouloir régler cette facture immédiatement après la livraison et nous sommes étonnés de n'avoir encore rien reçu.

Nous aimerions vous rappeler que nos conditions de paiement sont contre livraison des marchandises et que votre compte est en souffrance depuis deux mois.

Nous espérons que vous apprécierez notre situation. Comme vous ne nous avez pas fait connaître les raisons de ce retard, nous serons malheureusement obligés d'entamer des poursuites pour récupérer la somme due si nous ne recevons pas votre paiement avant le début du mois prochain.

Dans l'espoir d'une prompte réponse, veuillez agréer, Monsieur, nos salutations distinguées.

R. Duclos
Chef Comptable

(*Multilingual Business Handbook skeleton:* A6, E7, E9, E35, E52, E93, E125, E119, E113, A123)

Ashford International
26 Vicarage Road
Small Heath
BIRMINGHAM

Tel: (021) 771 2486

4 October 19

For the attention of Monsieur R. Duclos

Europ—Export
12 rue Kléber
67012 Strasbourg
France

Dear Sir

We acknowledge receipt of your invoice for the ten sets of crystal glasses and are sorry not to have replied sooner. We enclose a eurocheque in settlement of your invoice.

In fact the goods arrived in good condition in July and your second invoice arrived three weeks ago. The reason for the initial delay in payment was an oversight on the part of Mr Bennett who has now left our employment. The second delay has been because your second invoice was mislaid before my arrival a week ago.

We hope that you have not yet placed the matter in the hands of your lawyers and that this letter will render such action unnecessary.

Yours faithfully

Harvey Osborne
Chief Accountant

(*Multilingual Business Handbook skeleton:* A6, A9, A48, E80, E3, E100, E28, E115, E121)

Continue the preceding exchange of correspondence by composing a third letter (in French) on the basis of the following notes.

To: H. Osborne (Ashford International)

From: R. Duclos (Europ-Export)

- We have received your eurocheque.

- We are sorry about the apparent confusion in your company.

- We hope that business will henceforth be conducted in a more regular manner.

- Obviously we cannot wait several months for outstanding bills to be paid.

- Also very regrettably we had appraised our lawyers of the difficulties.

- We have obviously now told them that the problem has been solved. However there may be a small fee for work already done by them, which we would ask you to settle.

SECTION 5:   COMPLAINTS

This section is based on terms and expressions contained in Section F of the *MULTILINGUAL BUSINESS HANDBOOK*.

Touboulanger

3 rue de la Fontaine
16000 Angoulême

Tél: 45.92.50.14

Bakery Supplies Ltd
14 Bell Street
Walthamstow
London E11
Angleterre

Angoulême, le 14 mai 19

A l'attention de Monsieur Peter Fenwick

Monsieur,

Nous vous remercions de la rapide livraison de notre commande numéro 427 mais nous sommes au regret de devoir nous plaindre de votre expédition.

Malheureusement les tailles des moules à pâtisserie n'étaient pas toujours les bonnes; vous nous avez envoyé une grosse de taille 25 cm x 12,5 cm x 5 cm au lieu de 25 x 12,5 x 7,5. De plus les coloris des huches à pain émaillées ne sont pas conformes à notre commande; les huches émailleés bleu clair, que nous n'avons pas commandées, sont en plus éraflées et un peu rouillées.

Nous nous trouvons donc dans l'obligation de vous demander de nous envoyer des articles en remplacement aussitôt que possible et nous vous signalons que nous avons un besoin urgent de ces articles. Nous vous renvoyons immédiatement les articles non commandés et abîmés.

Nous vous prions d'agréer, Monsieur, l'expression de nos sentiments distingués.

Albert Lebon
Directeur Commercial

(*Multilingual Business Handbook skeleton:* A6, A1, F2, F5, F11, F4, F6, F22, F32, F35, F37, F43)

Bakery Supplies Ltd
14 Bell Street
Walthamstow
London E11

Tel: (01) 520 4977

23 May 19

Albert Lebon
Directeur Commercial
Touboulanger
3 rue de la Fontaine
16000 Angoulême
France

Dear Sir

Thank you for your letter of the 14th of this month. We are very sorry to learn that some of the baking tins in our consignment were of the wrong size and that some of the enamel breadbins were the wrong colour and scratched, or even slightly rusted.

We can only conclude that there was an error in our dispatching section and that the packaging materials were substandard. The items will certainly have to be replaced and we offer you our sincere apologies for this error.

If you have not already returned the defective breadbins may we suggest that you keep them and throw them away, or sell them off. We will in any case replace all the articles in question at our expense.

We hope to avoid similar errors in future.

Yours faithfully

Peter Fenwick
Managing Director

(*Multilingual Business Handbook skeleton:* A1, A10, A11, A22, F5, F4, F32, E27, F29, F47, F67, F42, F70, F48)

Continue the preceding exchange of correspondence by composing a third letter (in French) on the basis of the following notes.

To: Peter Fenwick (Bakery Supplies Ltd)

From: Albert Lebon (Touboulanger)

- Thank you for accepting our complaint.

- We managed to touch up and sell the breadbins at a reasonable price and owe you a proportion of the proceeds.

- We believe there is a growing market in France for certain types of traditional English food e.g. Eccles Cakes and Christmas Puddings.

- Can you supply moulds for making these items?

- Please send us details of price and specification.

- We would also be pleased to hear about any other traditional English foodstuffs you think the French might like.

Gérard Duverger   Tél: 78.37.29.44
Meubles de Luxe
5 Rue de la Bourse
69 LYON

Mr Gerald Stone
Roehampton Antiques
4 High Road
Roehampton
Surrey
Angleterre

Lyon, le 1er février 19

Mon cher Gerald

Je suis au regret de devoir me plaindre de votre expédition du 15 janvier. Le charmant bureau Chippendale a été abîmé par une manipulation peu soigneuse, semble-t-il. Il est arrivé assez endommagé – un des tiroirs est éraflé ainsi que le pied droit de devant. La douane française nous informe que cette avarie s'est vraisemblablement produite avant l'arrivée du bureau à Douvres.

Inutile, cher collègue, de vous demander de m'envoyer un remplacement aussitôt que possible, car cet article est presque irremplaçable. Je ne veux pas non plus vous renvoyer ce splendide meuble. Je voudrais par contre demander votre permission de le faire réparer par un ébéniste lyonnais et vous demander de me créditer pour le coût de la réparation.

Entretemps je vous conseille de vous adresser aux transitaires de Roehampton, puisque les avaries se sont produites en Grande-Bretagne. Veuillez trouver ci-joint la lettre de la douane française.

Je suis certain que cet incident regrettable vous attriste autant que moi, mais nous ne pouvons l'attribuer qu'à des circonstances imprévues et faire tout notre possible pour remettre ce bureau en état.

Toutes mes amitiés

Gérard Duverger
P.J. Lettre de la douane française

(*Multilingual Business Handbook skeleton:* F2, F19, F21, F33, F34, F35, F42, F57, F50, F60)

Roehampton Antiques
4 High Road
Roehampton
Surrey

(01) 700 0200

8 February 19

Gérard Duverger
Meubles de Luxe
5 Rue de la Bourse
69 Lyon
France

Dear Gérard

I was very upset to learn that the desk arrived in Lyon damaged. Please accept my most sincere apologies.

The desk must have been damaged in transit but it was not badly packed and the crate was not badly constructed in my opinion.

You inform me that the damage occurred between Roehampton Antiques and British Customs, and the letter you sent me confirms this. As the damage therefore occurred in transit in England, I shall contact the forwarding agents and take them to task. I shall also report the matter to my insurance company.

In the meantime, my dear Gérard, I would like you to organise the repair of the desk as you suggest and of course I accept full responsibility for the damage. Please deduct a suitable amount from our invoice and we will settle the details later.

Yours most sincerely

Gerald Stone

(*Multilingual Business Handbook skeleton:* F20, F67, F27, F28, F31, F33, A35, F60, F50, F79, F76, E18)

Continue the preceding exchange of correspondence by composing a third letter (in French) on the basis of the following notes.

To: Gerald Stone (Roehampton Antiques)

From: Gérard Duverger (Meubles de Luxe)

- Thank you for your sympathetic response to my letter.

- I have found a good repairer and fixed a good price (give details).

- The desk will be restored to its original pristine state.

- I enclose photographs of a fine Louis XIV escritoire.

- Also of a pair of bronze Boulle style lamps.

- Any interest?

SECTION 6:   AGENCIES

This section is based on terms and expressions contained in Section G of the *MULTILINGUAL BUSINESS HANDBOOK*.

Allard et Bouchon
Fabricants de Fenêtres
02100 St. Quentin

Tél: 23.62.77.69

> The Managing Director
> Black Country Double
> Glazing Severn Street
> Tipton
> West Midlands
> Angleterre

> St. Quentin, le 6 juin 19

Messieurs,

Suivant les recommandations de notre représentant britannique qui va bientôt prendre sa retraite, nous nous permettons de vous contacter parce que nous aimerions établir une agence pour vendre nos marchandises en Grande-Bretagne.

Cette agence doit accepter de ne pas travailler pour nos concurrents et doit limiter ses activités au pays mentionné ci-dessus.

Nous estimons que le potentiel de vente de nos produits, vitrages de tout genre simples ou doubles, est excellent et puisque nous avons appris que vous possédiez une expérience considérable dans la vente des portes et fenêtres à double vitrage, nous aimerions savoir si vous seriez intéressés à introduire nos marchandises sur le marché britannique.

Il va de soi que nous serions prêts à assurer la formation de vos représentants et à fournir les sommes nécessaires pour la publicité de notre produit.

Dans l'espoir d'une prompte réponse, nous vous prions d'agréer, Messieurs, l'expression de nos sentiments distingués.

Marielle Bouchon et Georges Allard
Directeurs

P.J. Catalogue des produits Allard et Bouchon

(*Multilingual Business Handbook skeleton*: A2, A21, G1, G5, G6, G13, G14, G15, G11, G20, A123, A127)

Black Country Double Glazing
Severn Street
Tipton
West Midlands

Tel: 021 253 8956

17 June 19

For the attention of Marielle Bouchon and Georges Allard

Allard et Bouchon
Fabricants de Fenêtres
02100 St. Quentin
France

Dear Sir and Madam

Thank you for your letter of the 6th of this month and for offering us the position as your agent in Great Britain.

We know some of your products and consider that they have excellent sales potential. We therefore wish to apply for the agency and we agree not to represent any of your competitors producing essentially the same articles.

Whilst we would also be prepared to advise on marketing and advertising in this country, where we have quite a large network of contacts, we should prefer to train our representatives ourselves. We are naturally prepared to take over the after-sales service.

In order to come to an agreement we will need to discuss various matters with you. For example, what will the duration of the agreement be and how can it be cancelled? Will your brochures be translated into English? What commission do you pay on orders and what expenses?

We look forward to an early reply or preferably a visit by one of your directors.

Yours faithfully

Eric Bateson

Proprietor

(*Multilingual Business Handbook skeleton:* A1, A4, A10, A11, G1, G13, G41, G47, G48, G49, G11, G45, G51, G53, G63, G81, G84, A123)

Continue the preceding exchange of correspondence by composing a third letter (in French) on the basis of the following notes.

To: E. Bateson (Black Country Double Glazing).

From: Marielle Bouchon (Allard et Bouchon)

- Thank you for your prompt reply and your interest in our proposal.

- We are pleased that you think our products have good potential in Great Britain.

- We will need to discuss the meaning of the phrase 'essentially the same articles'.

- My associate, Georges Allard, is coming to Britain next month and will be happy to visit you to discuss the questions you raise in your letter.

- We will telephone in a few days to arrange details of the visit.

Informatique Sans Frontières
73 rue Levallois
92500 Rueil Malmaison

Tél: 19.77.82.83

The Directors
Banana Computers Ltd
Blaenau Ffestiniog
Gwynedd
Pays de Galles

Paris, le 3 janvier 19

Messieurs,

Nous avons appris que vous cherchiez un représentant en France et puisque nous avons une grande expérience dans le domaine de l'informatique, nous voudrions vous offrir nos services pour cette représentation.

Nous ne sommes liés à aucune autre firme de votre pays et nous accepterions éventuellement de ne représenter aucun de vos concurrents britanniques. Par contre nous avons un contrat de représentation pour la vente des produits américains Business Computers Inc. et nous sommes les agents exclusifs des micro-ordinateurs de la société Computertechnik en RFA.

Nous avons de nombreux contacts en France et nous serions en mesure de vous conseiller en matière de publicité et de marketing pour la vente de vos appareils dans notre pays. Par exemple, il faudrait traduire vos brochures en français et nous pourrions nous occuper de cette traduction.

Veuillez nous faire savoir dans un délai d'un mois si notre proposition vous paraît intéressante. Tous les détails concernant les produits couverts par l'agence, le recrutement de représentants et le montant de commissions éventuelles seraient à régler lors d'une réunion de nos responsables.

Dans l'espoir d'une prompte réponse, nous vous prions d'agréer, Messieurs, l'expression de nos sentiments distingués.

Jean et Michel Despreux
Directeurs

(*Multilingual Business Handbook skeleton:* A2, G39, G40, G41, G46, G47, G60, G49, G48, G63, G65, G59, A123, A128)

Banana Computers
Blaenau Ffestiniog
Gwynedd
Wales

Tel: 0766 2432

21 January 19

For the attention of **M.M.** Despreux

Informatique Sans Frontières
73 rue Levallois
Rueil Malmaison
Paris
France

Dear Sirs

We acknowledge receipt of your letter of the 3rd inst. It is true that we are looking for an agent to sell our microcomputers in France.

Whilst we consider that these articles will find a ready market in your country, we nevertheless require a specialist representative. Can you assure us that you are experienced in this range of products?

We should be prepared to spend considerable sums on advertising, and our brochures will be translated into French. We would expect you to develop the French market for us in return for a commission of 7.5% of turnover. We would also expect to receive full details of any expenses that you wished us to pay, and commission and necessary expenses would normally be paid quarterly.

Please let us know within a month if these terms are acceptable to you.

Yours faithfully

David Thomas
Director

(*Multilingual Business Handbook skeleton:* A6, A2, A9, A11, G1, G38, G9, G40, G20, G63, G19, G87, G84, G90, G59)

Continue the preceding exchange of correspondence by composing a third letter (in French) on the basis of the following notes.

To: D. Thomas (Banana Computers)

From: Jean et Michel Despreux (Informatique Sans Frontières)

- We were one of the first retailers of microcomputers in France, now seven years ago.

- We formerly represented Gorgon Computers reasonably successfully until they went into liquidation.

- Below are the addresses of executives of Business Computers Inc. and Computertechnik who will attest to our competence and reliability.

- The terms that you propose as well as the question of expenses seem to us to be quite acceptable.

- It would be useful if one of our colleagues visited you or one of yours visited us to dot i's and cross t's. Could you suggest possible dates and venues?

SECTION 7:   REFERENCES

This section is based on terms and expressions contained in Section H of the *MULTILINGUAL BUSINESS HANDBOOK*.

Mondial Traductions
35 bis Rue Baudler
75013 Paris

Tél: 13.43.11.72

Linguacorps
4131 Oxford Street
LONDON
Angleterre

Paris, le 1er mai 19

A l'attention de Monsieur George Jones

Monsieur

Monsieur Alex Murphy a posé sa candidature à un poste de traducteur dans notre société et nous a donné votre nom comme référence. Nous vous serions très reconnaissants de bien vouloir nous fournir des renseignements sur son caractère et ses capacités.

Le travail de notre agence est très exigeant. Nous cherchons donc quelqu'un capable de s'adapter, honnête et assidu et connaissant bien les problèmes de la traduction technique.

Nous aimerions savoir pendant combien de temps Monsieur Murphy a travaillé pour vous, en quelle qualité il était employé et pour quelle raison il a quitté votre société. Nous vous prions de nous informer en outre s'il est d'une nature agréable, car le travail d'équipe est notre mode normal de travail.

Il va sans dire que nous considérerons tout renseignement fourni par vous comme strictement confidentiel.

Avec nos remerciements anticipés, nous vous prions d'agréer, Monsieur, l'expression de nos sentiments distingués.

Jean-Marie Escaboura
Secrétaire Général

(*Multilingual Business Handbook skeleton:* A6, A1, H1, H2, H4, H8, H9, H22, H12, H17, H16, H24, H10, A128)

Linguacorps
4131 Oxford Street
LONDON
Tel: (01) 511 7271

15 May 19

For the attention of Jean-Marie Escaboura

Mondial Traductions
35 bis Rue Baudler
75013 Paris
France

Dear Sir

Thank you for your letter of the 1st of this month. Mr Alex Murphy worked for us for 3 years until last December. He was totally reliable, honest and hardworking and had a very pleasant disposition.

He was trained by us as a teacher of English to foreign students and he was principally employed as a teacher. However he also did a number of technical translations for some of our customers and he began to develop a specialist knowledge of the electrical and electronic fields. His knowledge of French and German is excellent. He has always shown considerable initiative in his work.

He left us in December in order to marry a French national and it was his intention to settle in France. That is no doubt his reason for applying for a post with you. Since he carried out his duties to our complete satisfaction, we have no hesitation in recommending him as an excellent candidate.

Yours faithfully

George Jones

Director

(*Multilingual Business Handbook skeleton:* A6, A1, A10, A11, H11, H21, H22, H24, H14, H17, H25, H29, H27, H46, H47)

Continue the preceding exchange of correspondence by composing a third letter (in French) on the basis of the following notes.

To: G.T. Jones (Linguacorps)

From: J.M. Escaboura (Mondial Traductions)

- Thank you for the reference for Mr Murphy.

- We have now offered him a position. He seems to be a very good appointment.

- We have two propositions for you.

- Firstly, we have 2 or 3 firms whose translation work we do and who want to send some executives to learn English in England.

- Could you offer them intensive courses in Business English?

- Secondly, we would like to know whether you are interested in expanding your translation business, perhaps in partnership with us.

- Please inform when we could meet to discuss.

Etablissements Guillaume Levieux
Fromages Fins
4-9 Rue Levasseur
14000 Caen

Tél: 31.86.01.06

Dairy Marketing Board
4 Queensferry Street
BRISTOL
Avon
Angleterre

Caen, le 8 février 19

A l'attention de Mr John Smith

Monsieur

La société Mayfly Grocers (Dewsbury) Limited vient de nous confier une commande importante de quelques centaines de kilos de fromage. Elle a demandé que nous leur fassions crédit et nous a donné votre nom comme référence.

Etant donné que c'est la première fois que nous traitons avec cette maison, nous vous serions reconnaissants de bien vouloir nous donner des renseignements sur sa situation financière et sa réputation.

Nous serions également heureux de savoir depuis combien de temps vous connaissez cette maison, si vous entretenez des relations commerciales avec elle et si elle s'est toujours acquittée promptement de ses obligations. Nous aurions besoin de ces renseignements afin de pouvoir décider s'il serait prudent d'accorder un crédit important à cette maison.

Nous vous assurons que nous utiliserons vos renseignements avec la plus grande discrétion et que réciproquement nous serons toujours heureux de vous rendre le même service.

Dans l'espoir d'une prompte réponse, nous vous prions d'agréer, Monsieur, l'expression de nos sentiments amicaux.

Albert Levieux
Directeur Adjoint

(*Multilingual Business Handbook skeleton:* A6, A1, H55, H56, H58, H59, H65, H74, H77, H82, H89, H71, H72, H73, A123)

Dairy Marketing Board
Western Regional Office
4 Queensferry Street
Bristol
Avon

Tel: 0272 614 8732

14 February 19

For the attention of Albert Levieux

Etablissements Guillaume Levieux
Fromages Fins
4-9 Rue Levasseur
14000 Caen
France

Dear Sir

With reference to your letter of last week we have been doing business with Mayfly Grocers (Dewsbury) Ltd for some five years and we can assure you that the firm has an excellent reputation and is in a good financial position.

It has always fulfilled its obligations towards us promptly and we feel sure that you can allow the credit that you mention without qualms. The company has very considerable financial resources.

May we profit from this correspondence by asking you in turn whether you can give us any information about Monsieur André Letourneur, of 3 rue des Bosses, Suresnes? He has requested that we supply him with a large quantity of mature Cheddar cheese and asked for a credit term of 3 months. We would be most grateful for any information you can give us about the credit status and reliability of Mr Letourneur.

Yours faithfully

John Smith
General Manager

(*Multilingual Business Handbook skeleton:* A6, A1, A12, A11, H75, H78, H79, H82, H83, H80, H3, B116, H67)

Continue the preceding exchange of correspondence by composing a third letter (in French) on the basis of the following notes.

To: John Smith (Dairy Marketing Board (Bristol))

From: Albert Levieux (Ets. G. Levieux)

- Thank you for your reference regarding Mayfly Grocers.

- They have now promptly paid the first invoice and our trading relationship looks promising.

- We refer to our brief warning telex of 2 weeks ago concerning André Letourneur.

- As we suspected from our enquiries he is a very shady character.

- We hope you took notice of our warning and did not supply him with goods.

- In fact he has just been arrested and charged with fraud in several EEC countries.

SECTION 8: JOB APPLICATIONS AND ADVERTISEMENTS

This section is based on terms and expressions contained in Section I of the *MULTILINGUAL BUSINESS HANDBOOK*.

Exploitation Coopérative Fruitière

Tél: 75.04.04.55

Grand Mas du Pic Saint Loup
07110 Valflaunès

Department of Business Studies
The College of Higher Education
Bridgnorth
Shropshire
Angleterre

Valflaunès, le 3 mars 19

Messieurs,

Notre entreprise est une grande exploitation fruitière implantée dans le sud de la France. Sachant par notre Chambre de Commerce que vous formez des jeunes Britanniques en commerce international avec langues, nous vous informons que nous cherchons un jeune collaborateur pour notre service export.

La personne que nous recherchons devrait être capable de s'adapter à notre système et de travailler en équipe. Elle serait âgée de 20 ou 21 ans, et l'anglais serait sa langue maternelle. Une parfaite connaissance du français est essentielle et des connaissances d'allemand sont aussi souhaitées.

Nous sommes prêts à offrir un salaire de 6 500 francs par mois, avec treizième mois et 6 semaines de congés payés par an. Nous aiderons la personne recrutée à trouver un logement si besoin est.

Nous vous prions de faire connaître ces conditions à vos étudiants et de demander aux intéressés de nous envoyer une demande avec curriculum vitae et références.

Vous remerciant de votre coopération, nous vous prions d'agréer, Messieurs, l'expression de nos sentiments distingués.

Albert Ambault
Directeur du Personnel

(*Multilingual Business Handbook skeleton:* I1, I2, I7, I10, I17, I14, I13, I12, I20, I32, I31, I40, A127)

Department of Business Studies
The College of Higher Education
Bridgnorth
Shropshire

Tel: 0746 311522

12 March 19

For the attention of Mr Albert Ambault

Exploitation Coopérative Fruitière
Grand Mas du Pic Saint Loup
07110 Valflaunès
France

Dear Sir

I have learned from my lecturer, Mr Roger Welch, that you are looking for a young member of staff for your export department. I have received details of the post from Mr Welch and wish to apply for it.

As you will see from the enclosed curriculum vitae, I have some experience of work in an export department. I speak fluent French and German and wish to make use of my knowledge of these languages. I have already worked during a summer vacation in France and feel I can meet the requirements of this post.

I enclose a testimonial from my Head of Department, translated into French, and should be pleased to provide you with any other information you may require.

I can come for interview after 25 March and am available for work from 12 June onwards.

I hope you will consider my application favourably.

Yours faithfully

(*Multilingual Business Handbook skeleton:* A6, A1, I43, I2, I46, I45, I48, I49, I64, I51, I97, I107, I92, I95, I96)

Provide a curriculum vitae to accompany letter 8A2 using the format laid out in the appendix. The appendix also contains sample testimonials, which you may find it useful to consult.

Inter Décor
Papiers Peints et Tissus
8-10 rue de la République
59334 Tourcoing

Tél: 20.74.78.46

Northern Recruitment Limited
81 Piccadilly
Manchester
Angleterre

N/Réf: GR/AM/NR1

Tourcoing, le 4 avril 19

Messieurs,

Notre entreprise de textiles et de papiers peints est installée dans le nord de la France. Nous espérons que vous pourrez nous venir en aide car, pour remplacer 3 représentants qui quittent notre emploi, nous recherchons 3 représentants britanniques pour les régions nord-ouest, nord-est et centre de l'Angleterre.

Nous préférerions des personnes âgées de 25 à 35 ans, ayant au moins 5 ans d'expérience dans la vente des produits décoratifs. De plus, de bonnes connaissances de français sont souhaitées. Les candidats doivent pouvoir s'adapter aux besoins des différents clients et être en mesure de communiquer avec notre service export et nos dessinateurs.

Nous offrons une bonne rémunération en fonction de l'âge et de l'expérience des candidats ainsi qu'une généreuse commission. Les frais de déplacement en voiture sont entièrement remboursables. En plus, notre société dispose de son propre régime de retraite.

Veuillez avoir l'obligeance de nous envoyer les noms et coordonnées d'au moins 3 candidats avec références bancaires.

Dans l'espoir d'une prompte réponse, nous vous prions d'agréer, Messieurs, l'expression de nos meilleurs sentiments.

Geneviève Rochefort
Présidente

(*Multilingual Business Handbook skeleton:* I1, I6, I2, I10, I11, I12, I15, I18, I21, G77, I38, I39, I41, A123)

Northern Recruitment Limited
81 Piccadilly
Manchester
Tel: 061 763 8654

Your Ref: GR/AM/NR1
Our Ref: DP/5/com214

25 April 19

For the attention of Geneviève Rochefort

Inter Décor
Papiers Peints et Tissus
8-10 rue de la République
Tourcoing
France

Dear Madam

Thank you for your letter of 4 April with details of three posts in your company. This agency is pleased to send you the curricula vitae of three persons, two women and one man, who have considerable experience as representatives in the field of interior decoration products.

Miss Smyth is currently working for an export firm and is looking for a post which will enable her to make more use of her knowledge of French. Mr Terry would like to work for a larger organisation with international connections in order to improve his career prospects. Mrs Johnson wishes to change her job for personal reasons and is seeking a post with more responsibility.

We have interviewed these candidates, who all seem to have a pleasant disposition, though you yourself will have to judge their linguistic abilities. We have also received testimonials from previous employers in each case. As it is not our practice to ask clients to provide us with curricula vitae in foreign languages, I am asking the candidates to translate their c.v.'s into French and send them to you directly. Their c.v.'s will give the names of two referees to whom you can apply for further information. Mr Terry and Mrs Johnson would, however, be grateful if you did *not* approach their present employer without their prior consent.

If you wish to interview these candidates at our premises in Manchester we can arrange this for you.

Yours faithfully

Donald Pleasance

Director

(*Multilingual Business Handbook skeleton:* A6, A4, A10, A11, I46, I49, I11, I52, I53, I55, I56, I57, I54, I58, I59, H24, I97, G78, I100, I107, I102, I104, J5, A128)

Prepare a curriculum vitae and compose a short letter of application for one of the jobs referred to in letters 8B1 and 8B2. You may find it useful to consult the Appendix, which contains sample curricula vitae and testimonials.

SECTION 9: CHANGE OF ADDRESS etc.

This section is based on terms and expressions contained in Section J of the *MULTILINGUAL BUSINESS HANDBOOK*.

Précision Elvira
38 rue de l'Hôtel de Ville
69000 Lyon

Tél: 78.31.26.4(

Stones Jewellers Ltd
59 the Headrow
Leeds LS1 5LA
Yorkshire
England

Lyon, le 5 mai 19

Madame, Monsieur,

Nous avons le plaisir de vous informer qu'à la suite de la fusion de notre société avec la Société Aubin, certains détails pratiques sont à noter.

- à partir du 1er septembre nous serons connus sous le nouveau nom d' Elvira- Aubin.

- la production est transférée aux ateliers Aubin qui sont dotés des machines les plus modernes pour la fabrication de montres et horloges digitales et de chronomètres électroniques. Nous n'avons pas encore décidé si nous continuerons à assurer la fabrication de montres classiques à remontoir.

- les bureaux de la nouvelle société seront situés au siège social de l'ancienne société Elvira où toute correspondance devra être adressée.

- par contre, à partir du 1er septembre toute marchandise doit être expédiée à notre société associée dont l'adresse est la suivante:

> Société Elvira-Aubin
> 50 rue Lecourbe
> 69000 Lyon

Nous vous prions de prendre bonne note de ces détails et d'informer votre service d'expédition de ce changement d'adresse. Soyez assurés que nous maintiendrons la même haute qualité de nos services.

Nous serons très heureux de vous faire bénéficier de ces améliorations et vous prions de croire, Madame, Monsieur, à nos sentiments les plus dévoués.

P. Darbois
Secrétaire Général

(*Multilingual Business Handbook skeleton:* A32, J17, J24, J5, J10, J17, J28, J9, J11, J7)

Stones Jewellers Ltd
59 The Headrow
Leeds LS1 5LA
Yorkshire

Tel: (0)532 647234

12 May 19

For the attention of M. Darbois

Précision Elvira
38 rue de l'Hôtel de Ville
69000 Lyon
France

Dear Sir

Thank you for your letter of 5 May. We note that you have merged with the Société Aubin and have informed our dispatch department of your new name and address. Whilst we hope that the merger will be of benefit to both companies, we deeply regret that you seem to be considering ceasing production of clockwork timepieces and specialising only in the manufacture of digital and electronic watches. In our view traditional timepieces still have excellent sales potential, probably as a reaction to the flood of electronic watches, and we wonder if this has been properly taken into account.

We therefore hope that you will understand our position and that, given the considerable and continuing demand for these goods, you will continue to manufacture classical clockwork timepieces post-merger.

In the hope of an early reply, we remain

Yours faithfully

Albert Stone
Director

(*Multilingual Business Handbook skeleton:* A10, A11, A44, J16, J11, J17, A43, J20, J21, G13, A90, A88, J19, A123)

Continue the preceding exchange of correspondence by composing a third letter (in French) on the basis of the following notes.

To: Albert Stone (Stones Jewellers Ltd)

From: M. Darbois (Précision Elvira)

- Thank you for your letter of 12th inst.

- The situation is clearer now and we regret that the production of clockwork timepieces will cease from Sept. 1.

- We will however continue to offer a full spare parts and after-sales service on our present models.

- Our intention is to produce only luxury digital watches.

- Our modern machinery should result in competitive prices and we shall be pleased to offer you a discount of 5% on future orders in view of our longstanding business relations.

Etablissements Tramel
Matériel pour Ordinateurs
3 rue de la Batellerie
44000 Nantes

Tél: 40.74.70.15

Specialist Computers Ltd
1112 Corporation Street
Birmingham
England

Nantes, le 24 mai 19

N/Réf: JLD/ETR286

A l'attention de Mr B Rourke

Monsieur,

A la suite de notre commande no. 7429 du 25 novembre 19.., nous avons reçu livraison de 25 micro-ordinateurs COMPTEL, avec la possibilité de reprise des invendus. Notre clientèle s'est tout d'abord très peu intéressée à ces appareils, du fait que le COMPTEL n'est pas compatible IBM. Cependant la vente courante a rapidement progressé et il semble maintenant que le potentiel de vente de ces articles est excellent.

Ce renversement de situation est la conséquence directe d'une augmentation de la demande de la part des établissements d'enseignement qui ont trouvé que le COMPTEL leur offrait une gamme très étendue de logiciel pédagogique à des prix très modérés. C'est en partie grâce à l'importance de nos investissements publicitaires que l'Enseignement Assisté par Ordinateur (EAO) est à l'heure actuelle une industrie de pointe en France.

Nous sommes donc heureux de vous informer que nous serons bientôt à court de stock et que nous désirons vous confier la commande suivante:

    30 micro-ordinateurs COMPTEL
    15 moniteurs couleur COMPCOL
    15 moniteurs monochrome COMPMON
     5 modems COMPMOD2
    10 imprimantes matricielles COMPDOT

Nous aurions besoin de ces articles d'ici 10 jours et nous espérons donc que vous pourrez nous les livrer sur stock.

Nous vous serions reconnaissants de bien vouloir nous donner confirmation de cette commande et vous prions d'agréer, Monsieur, l'expression de nos sentiments distingués.

Jean-Luc Delon
Chef des Achats

(*Multilingual Business Handbook skeleton:* A14, A6, A1, A29, C17, Q7, B50, Q60, G13, Q70, Q50, B18, C6, Q107, Q106, Q36, Q113, C14, C13, A127)

Messrs Grace & Jones
Accountants
5 Paradise Square
Birmingham BM1 2SL

Tel: 021 375 4289

Your Ref: JLD/ETR286

Our Ref: SG/KF/D2.ET

29 May 19

For the attention of Mr J-L Delon

Etablissements Tramel
Matériel pour Ordinateurs
3 rue de la Bataillerie
44000 Nantes
France

Re: Your letter of 24 May

Dear Sir

We acknowledge receipt of the above-mentioned letter and regret to inform you that Specialist Computers Ltd ceased trading 2 months ago. The company is bankrupt and the receiver has been called in. Mr Rourke himself has moved to another company.

Attempts are being made to salvage parts of the company but the manufacture of machines which are not IBM compatible will not be continued. Indeed, the company's bankruptcy was in large part due to its over-reliance on the COMPTEL range of computers and peripherals, which were never industry standard and which are now generally regarded as obsolete.

We very much regret that Specialist Computers Ltd can no longer supply the market for Computer Aided Learning which you have evidently spent considerable sums of money in developing, and hope you will be able to find another supplier.

Yours faithfully

Steven Grace
Partner

(*Multilingual Business Handbook skeleton:* A9, A25, A31, J32, J33, J34, J41, Q60, Q105, B57, A43, Q50, G19, C23)

Continue the preceding exchange of correspondence by composing a third letter (in French) on the basis of the following notes:

To: Messrs Grace & Jones (Accountants)

From: J-L Delon (Etablissements Tramel)

- We read with dismay the contents of your letter of 29 May.

- You will appreciate we have spent over 100,000 francs promoting COMPTEL computers and are now being denied the opportunity to reap the rewards of that investment.

- Can you please provide the following information:

    — will spares continue to be available?

    — are there any stocks of computers remaining subsequent to the declaration of bankruptcy?

    — will production of COMPTEL computers be taken over by another company?

    — is there a parent or associated company we could contact about this matter?

SECTION 10: TRAVEL AND HOTEL RESERVATIONS

This section is based on terms and expressions contained in Section K of the *MULTILINGUAL BUSINESS HANDBOOK*.

Agence Internationale Hermès
5 Avenue Marceau
75007 PARIS

Tél: 45.51.10.46
Télex: 27116

Rogers Engineering Ltd
87 Mildmay Road
Chelmsford
Essex
Angleterre

Paris, le 10 février 19

Monsieur et cher client,

Nous accusons réception de votre réponse à notre annonce dans l'édition de la semaine dernière de l'hebdomadaire Business Weekly et vous en remercions.

A la suite de cette demande de renseignements nous vous proposons notre voyage organisé PARIS-FOLIES qui nous semble répondre le mieux aux besoins que vous mentionnez, c'est-à-dire: à titre d'encouragement, offrir un séjour à Paris aux représentants de votre société ayant réalisé les meilleures ventes de l'année.

Ce voyage organisé comprend:

— vol charter le vendredi après-midi de Ashford dans le Kent à Beauvais dans l'Oise, 75 kilomètres au nord-ouest de Paris, où l'un de nos agents assurera l'accueil des voyageurs. Des rafraîchissements seront servis pendant le vol.
— car spécial de Beauvais à Paris
— réception au champagne à l'arrivée à l'hôtel qui est proche du centre-ville
— chambres à deux lits avec douche et W.C.
— pension complète, y compris banquet offert en l'honneur de la société le samedi soir
— retour à Beauvais en car spécial et retour en avion à Ashford le dimanche après-midi

Les tarifs par personne sont de 1800 F pendant la haute-saison et de 1600 F au début de la saison ou à l'arrière-saison. Le voyage organisé PARIS-FOLIES est également offert au tarif réduit de 1500 F du 1er au 21 février. Nos prix sont tout compris.

Nous sommes à votre disposition pour vous fournir tout renseignement supplémentaire, le cas échéant, et vous prions d'agréer, Monsieur et cher client, l'expression de nos sentiments les meilleurs.

J. Tournier
Directeur Commercial

(*Multilingual Business Handbook skeleton:* E1, I44, C3, K46, K58, K10, K94, K63, K65, K80, K10, K67, K68, K69, K70)

Rogers Engineering
187 Mildmay Road
Chelmsford
Essex

Tel: 0245 374838

18 February 19

For the attention of Mr J. Tournier

Agence Internationale Hermès
5 Avenue Marceau
75007 Paris
France

Dear Sir

Thank you for sending us details of your PARIS-FOLIES package. We are interested in the package and would be pleased to receive the following information:

1. At what time on Friday does the plane leave Ashford and how long before departure must passengers check in?

2. Is a meal included in the refreshments served during the flight? We feel this will be necessary, as participants will have already have been travelling for some time when they arrive at Ashford.

3. Can you offer a discount for a group of about 12 people?

4. Will it be possible to organise a visit to a typical Parisian night club on the Friday evening?

For your information, the weekend we have in mind for the trip is that of 18 March.

Yours faithfully

John Mason

Sales Director

(*Multilingual Business Handbook skeleton:* B35, A106, K45, K49, K59, K58, K50, K43)

Continue the preceding exchange of correspondence by composing a third letter (in French) on the basis of the following notes.

To: John Mason (Rogers Engineering)

From: J. Tournier (Agence Internationale Hermès)

- I am pleased to provide the information you require.

- The plane leaves Ashford at 4.00 p.m. local time and passengers are requested to check in 1.5 hours before departure.

- The refreshments do not normally include a full meal as the flight is quite short, but we could provide a cold collation for you.

- It is our normal practice to only offer a discount for groups of 20+ but we can offer you an introductory discount of 5%.

- We could arrange a visit to a nightclub, but this would mean increasing the price of the package by about 300 francs per person.

Cuisine-Equipement
42 rue Vivienne
75002 Paris

Tél: 47.42.53.33

Centre Point Hotel
309 Hagley Road
Edgbaston
Birmingham
Angleterre

A l'attention de Mr P. Rooney

Paris, le 13 mars 19

Monsieur,

Votre nom nous a été donné par la Chambre de Commerce de Birmingham à qui nous avions demandé de nous recommander un hôtel aménagé pour recevoir un congrès international et pourvoir à ses besoins.

Notre société est une société internationale qui se spécialise dans la fabrication de cuisines intégrées de haute gamme. Nous avons l'intention d'exposer nos articles lors de la foire commerciale qui aura lieu au National Exhibition Centre du 27 au 30 juin et d'associer cet événement à une réunion de nos directeurs des ventes à Birmingham du 30 juin au 3 juillet.

Il est difficile de vous donner pour le moment le nombre exact de participants. Nous estimons à 16 le nombre de membres de notre siège social à Paris et à environ 10 ceux de nos sociétés associées de toute l'Europe, qui pourraient faire partie de cette réunion. Comme nous prévoyons également l'arrivée de représentants de diverses chambres de commerce, de sociétés d'exploitation ainsi que la présence d'hommes d'affaires de la région qui envisageraient d'obtenir un contrat de franchise pour la vente de nos articles en Grande-Bretagne, le nombre de participants pourrait varier de 16 à 40 selon le moment.

C'est pourquoi nous recherchons un hôtel qui soit à même de faire face à un nombre imprécis de clients et qui puisse s'adapter à leurs besoins, tout en offrant un service de très haute qualité. Nous voudrions également savoir si vos salles de conférences sont disponibles pendant la période mentionnée ci-dessus. Nous aimerions aussi qu'un car vienne chercher les participants à l'aéroport de Birmingham. Il se peut que nous cherchions à organiser des excursions en car à la ville neuve de Telford dans le Shropshire.

Dans le cas où il vous serait possible de satisfaire à nos besoins, veuillez nous envoyer des renseignements complets sur votre hôtel et la liste de vos prix.

Dans l'espoir d'une prompte réponse, nous vous prions d'agréer, Monsieur, nos meilleures salutations.

D. Kefalek
Directeur Commercial

(*Multilingual Business Handbook skeleton:* A15, B2, B25, K70, J1, J28, G27, G2, I15, K92, K74, B5, A123)

Centre Point Hotel
309 Hagley Road
Edgbaston
Birmingham B1L 7WS
England

Tel: (0)21 426 7984
426 7341

Telex: CENPOT 234500

21 March 19

Cuisine-Equipement
42 rue Vivienne
F-75002 Paris
France

Dear Mr Kefalek

Thank you for your letter of 13 March. We have over 10 years' experience in hosting international conferences and would be pleased to accept a group booking for 30 June to 3 July. I do not think that the changing number of participants would create any difficulties, as the local representatives of the business community and Chambers of Commerce who come to the meeting would probably choose to return home in the evening, rather than spend the night in our hotel. In the circumstances I would be prepared to guarantee the availability of 20 rooms for the 3 nights and would obviously do my best to accommodate any 'extras'. There is certainly no problem numbers-wise as far as conference rooms are concerned, as our largest room can take up to 100 people and is available for the dates you require.

I doubt whether it is necessary for participants to be picked up by coach from the airport, particularly as they may well be arriving at different times. There is a station at Birmingham International Airport and a fast Intercity train service to Birmingham New Street. The hotel is a 5 minute taxi ride from New Street station. For participants arriving by car the hotel is close to the centre of town and has its own car park. We have established links with a local coach firm and can organise an excursion to Telford.

I am enclosing our brochure and price list as requested and hope to have been of help to you.
Yours sincerely

Paul Rooney
Assistant Manager

Encs: Brochure, price list

(Multilingual Business Handbook skeleton: A10, A11, I11, K71, K70, F49, A120, K76, K92, K93, K74, K94, K87, A34, A70, A124, A129)

Continue the preceding exchange of correspondence by composing a third letter (in French) on the basis of the following notes.

To: Paul Rooney (Centre Point Hotel)

From: D. Kefalek (Cuisine-Equipement)

- Thank you for your very detailed letter, brochure and price list.

- We have a clearer idea of the number of 'full-time' participants now and would like to reserve 18 single rooms with shower and toilet for the period 30 June – 3 July.

- Could you keep 2 other rooms as 'standbys', as suggested.

- Participants will take all meals in the hotel.

- We will require a conference room with video and projection facilities from 9 a.m. on the 1st to 1.00 p.m. on 3 July.

- Participants will be leaving during the afternoon of the 3rd.

- Most of them will be taking the afternoon flight to Paris, so a coach to the airport will be required on this occasion.

- Please let me know your normal arrangements for payment.

SECTION 11: PROPERTY: SALES AND RENTALS

This section is based on terms and expressions contained in Section L of the *MULTILINGUAL BUSINESS HANDBOOK*.

Fabrication Electro-Ménagère

Tél: 85.38.00.77

15 rue du Fer-à-Moulin
71000 Mâcon

Swallows Estate Agents
(Commercial & Industrial)
Lulworth Garth
Leeds LS1 7SG
Angleterre

Mâcon, le 30 janvier 19

Monsieur,

Articulated lorry

Par suite de la croissance régulière de nos affaires en Grande-Bretagne, nous avons décidé d'établir à Leeds une petite installation industrielle et commerciale. Nous recherchons des locaux d'environ 3500 m2 qui conviendraient aux besoins d'une industrie légère et offriraient également une surface adéquate pour les bureaux. Les semi-remorques devraient pouvoir accéder à ces locaux dont la localisation idéale serait entre les autoroutes M1 et M62 et de préférence dans une zone industrielle. Pourriez-vous nous faire savoir si de tels locaux sont disponibles et nous renseigner sur le montant mensuel du loyer.

Monsieur Maurer, notre architecte, a l'intention de surveiller l'installation de cette nouvelle usine, par contre, nous envisageons de recruter une main d'oeuvre locale.

Monsieur Maurer souhaiterait louer une maison meublée dans la zone verte du sud de Leeds. Nous sommes prêts à payer une location de £300 maximum par mois pour une maison individuelle et serions heureux de savoir si de telles propriétés sont disponibles dans la région.

Dans l'espoir d'une prompte réponse, nous vous prions d'agréer, Monsieur, nos meilleures salutations.

R. Samardet
Directeur Général

(*Multilingual Business Handbook skeleton:* J4, L18, L14, L12, C8, L20, L7, A123)

Swallows Estate Agents
(Commercial & Industrial)
Lulworth Garth
Leeds LS1 7SG

Tel: 0532 764921

Fabrication Electro-Ménagère
15 rue du Fer-à-Moulin   8 February 1?
71000 Mâcon
France

Dear Mr Samardet

We thank you for your letter of 30 January.

The Leeds City Council has adopted a policy of urban renewal for some time now and this has resulted in the creation of a number of inner-city industrial estates. Several of our clients have recently expressed interest in a small industrial estate which has been built in Hunslet and these expressions of interest lead us to believe that it may be a good location for the kind of commercial and industrial unit you describe.

Hunslet is only a few minutes from the city centre and about 2 miles from the start of the M1, which crosses the M62 some miles to the south. The roads between the M1 and the Hunslet industrial estate are good and articulated lorries can gain easy access to the estate itself.

For premises of 3,500 m² you would expect to pay in the region of £5.00 per m².

As for Mr Maurer's house, we have several which may be suitable but the rents vary considerably. I am sending you our current property list by the same post.

I hope to have been of help to you and that you will write again if I can be of service in any way.

Yours sincerely

Christopher Ackroyd
Industrial Section

Encs: Property list

(*Multilingual Business Handbook skeleton:* A10, A11, B9, L21, K97, A50, A52, A124, A95, A129)

Continue the preceding exchange of correspondence by composing a third letter (in French) on the basis of the following notes.

To: C. Ackroyd (Swallows Estate Agents)

From: R. Samardet (Fabrication Electro-Ménagère)

• Thank you for your letter of 8 February.

• We are very interested in the Hunslet Industrial Estate and would like to visit it as soon as possible.

• Mr Maurer is currently on a business trip but I will ask him to ring you upon his return in order to organise a trip to Leeds before the end of February.

• The property best suited to Mr Maurer's own needs seems to be the detached 4 bedroomed house with a garage in Plough Lane, Thrape.

• Is is still free and would it be possible to rent it for 6 months rather than one year?

CODIM
Compagnie de
Développement Immobilier
18 rue Jean-Jacques Rousseau
38000 Grenoble

Tél: 76.55.07.91
Télex: 27240 CODIM F.

Sunseekers Estate Agents
1117 The Broadway
Ealing
London W5
Angleterre

Grenoble, le 5 avril 19

Monsieur,

A la suite de la mise en valeur du domaine de Lombrez dans le sud-ouest de la France, notre société a entrepris la construction d'appartements et de maisons individuelles de haut standing dans ce domaine et nous recherchons un agent pour vendre ces propriétés sur le marché britannique où nous avons de fortes raisons de croire que la demande est élevée, surtout en vue de la construction du tunnel sous la Manche.

Votre tâche principale serait de présenter nos catalogues à des clients éventuels et il vous incomberait la responsabilité de les inclure dans la composition des étalages de toutes vos agences. Il va sans dire que nous fournirons ces catalogues en anglais.

Les différentes catégories de logements à vendre sont les suivantes:

Appartements
— charmantes studettes. kitchen. salle d'eau. Prix: 300 000 F
— studios. charme. calme. placards muraux dans le couloir. balcon. terrasse.
  Prix: 420 000 F
— grands 4 pièces. tout confort. panorama. parking sous-sol. Prix: 690 000 F

Maisons
— charmantes maisons. séjour. cuisine. bains. jardin clos. 2/3 chambres. Prix: 950 000 F
— belles maisons 600m2. 5 pièces. Prix: 1 350 000 F
— superbes villas (2 seulement). living. 6 chambres. 3 bains. cave. garage. 1 ha.
  Prix: 2 300 000 F

(Prêts disponibles à un taux d'intérêt avantageux)

.../...

Toutes ces propriétés sont garanties 5 ans y compris une garantie contre les malfaçons de 1 an. Elles sont situées sur un emplacement très attrayant dans un nouveau village de vacances près de Port Barcarès, à proximité de Perpignan. Nous avons organisé des vols d'inspection gratuits de Gatwick à Perpignan pour les futurs acquéreurs que vous jugeriez particulièrement intéressés.

Nous sommes prêts à vous confier cette représentation à titre d'essai en premier lieu, pour ensuite reconsidérer la situation six mois plus tard. La commission habituelle pour nos représentants à l'étranger est de 2%, payable sur toutes les ventes conclues par vous ou vos intermédiaires.

Nous serions heureux de savoir aussitôt que possible si cette proposition vous intéresse et nous restons à votre disposition pour vous fournir de plus amples renseignements.

Veuillez agréer, Monsieur, nos salutations distinguées.

R. Hardouin
Directeur de Promotion

(*Multilingual Business Handbook skeleton:* L5, G1, G7, G71, L26, L27, L21, L34, G50, G56, G79, G80)

Sunseekers Estate Agents
1117 The Broadway
Ealing
London W5

Tel: 01 997 7932

CODIM
Compagnie de Développement Immobilier   12 April 19
18 rue Jean-Jacques Rousseau
38000 Grenoble
France

Dear Mr Hardouin

We thank you for your letter of 5 April offering us an agency agreement for your properties in S.W. France. We have successfully represented a number of property development companies in the past and specialise in the sale of second and retirement homes in warm climates.

We would be prepared to accept the agency for 6 months on a trial basis, on the following conditions:

1. Your catalogue would be included in the window displays of all our agencies, as per your request.

2. You would send us the catalogues in French but we would arrange translation at our expense and generally advise on marketing and advertising in this country.

3. Since we are prepared to take on part of the cost of advertising, we would require a commission of 2.5% on properties costing less than 500,000 francs and of 3% on properties costing in excess of 500,000 francs, the commission to be paid upon conclusion of the sale.

4. You would pay for all free inspection flights, even if the client does not purchase a property.

5. Loans would normally be arranged through our insurance company.

At a more general level, we are impressed by the range of properties available, particularly at the upper end of the market. We wonder, however, if you have considered the possibility of time-sharing, as this is becoming increasingly popular in Britain and would open the market to a much greater number of potential clients.

We would welcome your views on this matter and on the above points and remain,

Yours sincerely,

Steven Hardy

(*Multilingual Business Handbook skeleton:* A10, A11, G60, G61, G42, J21, G56, B71, G71, G67, G65, G48, G73, G91, L34, L32, A72)

Continue the preceding exchange of correspondence by composing a third letter (in French) on the basis of the following notes.

To: S. Hardy (Sunseekers Estate Agents)

From: R. Hardouin (CODIM)

- The conditions you propose are acceptable to us, with the exception of nos 3 and 5.

- We are not prepared to offer a commission of more than 2.5% across the board.

- As far as condition 5 is concerned, the word 'normally' is imprecise. We would not accept that loans would always be arranged by yourselves.

- We suggest a compromise whereby the final choice is left to the client himself, according to the offers made to him.

- Your concept of time-sharing is very interesting and we need to discuss it further.

SECTION 12:   FINANCIAL REPORTS

This section is based on terms and expressions contained in Section M of the *MULTILINGUAL BUSINESS HANDBOOK*.

Société J. Bressane
Equipement Electro-Ménager
140 Avenue de Fronton
31200 TOULOUSE

Tél: 61.47.61.01

Bressane (UK)
Wharf St. Works
Halifax HA4 7WS
Angleterre

Toulouse, le 10 octobre 19

Cher Brian,

A la suite d'une réunion que j'ai eue avec le Président et le Directeur Commercial de notre société, j'espère que vous pourrez nous venir en aide au cours des 2 ou 3 mois qui suivent, si, comme nous le prévoyons, les objectifs de production ne peuvent être atteints et que nous soyons obligés de pallier à une baisse de production inévitable.

Cette situation résulte d'un ensemble d'éléments: manque de personnel, modernisation de nos ateliers à la suite de notre programme d'investissement à long terme et ventes intérieures exceptionnellement soutenues pour cette période de l'année. Nous utilisons nos ressources disponibles au maximum mais nous prévoyons peu à peu du retard sur la production et nous serons bientôt à court de marchandises.

Si cette tendance continue, nous prévoyons que les articles suivants nous manqueront:

moteurs de machine à laver LB206 –	1000 unités par mois
interrupteurs de contrôle IC20 –	500 unités par mois
gros tuyaux de caoutchouc TC12 –	1000 unités par mois

Il me semble que dans de telles circonstances la seule façon de remédier à cette augmentation imprévue de la demande est de transférer la production supplémentaire à votre usine qui, si je ne me trompe, ne produit pas à plein rendement à l'heure actuelle.

Je me rends compte que cet appel pourrait vous occasionner des difficultés considérables mais nous avons besoin de ces articles afin de conserver notre place de leader dans le secteur des machines à laver.

Il va sans dire que nous serions prêts à vous rendre le même service si vous vous trouviez dans une situation semblable.

Dans l'espoir que vous me répondrez par l'affirmative, je vous envoie mes meilleures amitiés.

Jean-Paul Sarraute
Directeur

(Multilingual Business Handbook skeleton: M9, M11, M12, M47, M41, M45, C37, J25, F36, M46)

Bressane (UK)
Wharf Street Works
Halifax HA4 7WS
Yorkshire

Tel: (0422) 563 2291

20 October 19

Société J. Bressane
Equipement Electro-Ménager
140 Avenue de Fronton
31200 Toulouse
France

Dear Jean-Paul

Thank you for your letter of the 10th of this month. I am pleased to hear that sales are so buoyant and regret that you are meeting difficulties with production. I would like to point out straight away that since the Chairman presented the report for the last financial year, we have increased production by 8% and are now working at close to full capacity. In order to produce the extra goods you require, we would have to create new jobs, leading to increased staffing costs. This would no doubt be noted at next year's A.G.M.

In brief, then, Jean-Paul, I would like to help you out but require assurance that the extra costs incurred will not be held against us in this year's financial report.

Yours sincerely

Brian Hartley
Director

(*Multilingual Business Handbook skeleton:* A10, A11, A19, M68, A78, M22, M24, M27, M77, M3, M22)

Continue the preceding exchange of correspondence by composing a third letter (in French) on the basis of the following notes.

To: Brian Hartley (Bressane UK)

From: Jean-Paul Sarraute (Bressane France)

- Thank you for your letter and kind offer of help.

- The Board met yesterday and agreed that your point was a reasonable one.

- The Chairman has agreed to explain the situation at the next A.G.M.

- I trust you will now be able to proceed to take on the extra staff you need in order to ensure that the first consignment of goods reaches us by 15 November at the latest.

Ingénierie Falgarde
40 Route de Turin
06000 NICE

Tél: 93.89.10.74

Falgarde (Scotland)
Maritime Works
Irvine
Ayrshire
ECOSSE

Nice, le 8 juillet 19

Cher John,

Au cours de notre Assemblée Générale Annuelle, qui, comme vous le savez, a eu lieu le 3 juillet, nous avons remarqué qu'au cours de l'exercice précédent les ventes totales du groupe ont baissé de 9,5% par suite de circonstances commerciales déplorables.

Les bénéfices de la Société ont fortement diminué durant le dernier trimestre et aucun dividende n'a été versé. Le Conseil d'Administration reconnaît à présent qu'un certain nombre de décisions pénibles doivent être prises afin de sauvegarder l'avenir de la Société.

Je regrette de devoir vous informer qu'une des solutions proposées au Conseil entraînerait la fermeture de nos filiales européennes les moins rentables et qu'il est probable que vous seriez concerné au cas où cette solution serait choisie.

Le Conseil comprend que la situation économique actuelle ne vous a pas été d'un grand secours pour sortir des difficultés créées par la restructuration entreprise l'année dernière. Dans l'ensemble, on pense que la conjoncture britannique est en surprospérité et le Conseil comprend fort bien que la solidité de la livre sterling a eu un effet nuisible sur les exportations. Inversement, si le Chancelier de l'Echiquier s'efforce de réduire la consommation domestique en augmentant le taux d'intérêt sur les prêts, il est probable que les ventes intérieures en souffriraient et que la situation de la filiale britannique ne serait guère meilleure.

Je vous fais part de la façon de penser du Conseil d'Administration pour que vous ayez amplement le temps de préparer les arguments que vous présenteriez devant le prochain Conseil en faveur de la continuation du fonctionnement de votre usine. La prochaine réunion du Conseil aura lieu au siège social de la Société le 24 juillet et vous serez invité à y participer. Je suis certain qu'un grand nombre de mes collègues s'associeraient à moi pour vous souhaiter de réussir dans votre plaidoyer en faveur de l'usine d'Irvine.

Mes amitiés,

O. Garac
Secrétaire Administratif

(*Multilingual Business Handbook skeleton:* M3, M22, M43, M62, M57, M19, A31, M73, M1)

Falgarde (Scotland)
Maritime Works
Irvine
Ayrshire

Mr O Garac
Ingénierie Falgarde
140 Route de Turin
06000 Nice
France

Tel: 0294 590 344

17 July 19

Dear Olivier

Thank you for communicating the Board's thinking to me. I am of course extremely sorry to learn that the Board is considering closing the Irvine plant but am confident that the case I shall make for its continuing operation is a convincing one.

The main points I shall be making are as follows:

1. The Irvine plant is far from being the least profitable European subsidiary. The losses announced by the Spanish and Italian subsidiaries were particularly heavy in the last financial year.

2. Our strategy has been to sacrifice short-term profits for medium-term growth and we expect an increase in our total business over the next 3 years.

3. The restructuring undertaken last year was a key part of our long-term investment programme, to which the Board itself agreed.

4. Historically, our largest markets have always been Denmark and Sweden; the strong pound has reduced demand very considerably in these countries, especially in the second half of this year. However, we are of the opinion that this situation is unlikely to continue indefinitely.

5. Conversely, there has been a favourable development in our domestic sales, which have risen by 17%.

6. Closure of the Irvine plant would be a disaster for the local economy, which already suffers from a high rate of unemployment.

I would welcome your views on these points and look forward to seeing you at the meeting of 24 July.

Yours sincerely

John Green
Director

(*Multilingual Business Handbook skeleton:* A22, M79, M22, M50, M51, M52, M47, M39, M65, M66, M40, M55, M43, A72)

Continue the preceding exchange of correspondence by composing a third letter (in French) on the basis of the following notes.

To: John Green (Falgarde Scotland)

From: Olivier Garac (Ingénierie Falgarde)

- Thanks for your letter. I appreciated the optimistic tone.

- The date of the Board Meeting has been changed to 31 July.

- The M.D. will be visiting the Spanish subsidiary during the previous week.

- At least the M.D. will know what he's talking about after his visit to Spain.

- If I were you, the two points I would most stress would be: (1) you are far from being the least profitable European subsidiary, and (2) that domestic sales *are* rising. This is important because the Irvine plant was intended to supply the UK domestic market, rather than export to Scandinavian countries.

- I fear that the likely effects of closure on the local economy would not carry much weight.

- Best wishes etc.

SECTION 13:   BANK AND POST OFFICE

This section is based on terms and expressions contained in Section O of the *MULTILINGUAL BUSINESS HANDBOOK*.

12 Chemin des Abricotiers
La Tronche
38700 Corenc

> Monsieur le Directeur
> Bridgers Bank Ltd
> King Street
> Telford
> Shropshire
> Angleterre

> Corenc, le 13 juillet 19

Monsieur,

Votre nom m'a été donné par Mr Davies, Directeur du Personnel de Telfex Ltd., pour qui je travaillerai pour 6 mois à partir du 1er septembre. Comme mon salaire sera versé en Angleterre, j'aimerais ouvrir un compte courant et un compte de dépôts à votre banque à dater du 15 août. J'ai déjà un compte en France à la BRG (Banque Régionale de Grenoble), Square des Postes, Grenoble. Le numéro de mon compte est 06132152 et le directeur de cette branche, M. Jourdan, est prêt à vous fournir des références.

Je crois savoir que les frais de banque ne sont pas comptés si le solde n'est pas à découvert de même que les chéquiers, cartes bancaires et relevés de compte mensuels sont émis gratuitement. Je n'aurai besoin de faire appel à vous pour aucun règlement spécial, bien que j'espère faire de temps en temps des virements bancaires d'Angleterre en France et vice-versa et j'aimerais savoir combien de jours une telle transaction prend dans chaque direction.

Pourriez-vous également me dire de quelle façon je peux obtenir l'équivalent anglais de la Carte Bleue de crédit française, et s'il y a un distributeur automatique de billets (DAB) dans votre banque.

Dans l'espoir que l'ouverture de ce compte ne présentera aucune difficulté et que je recevrai bientôt votre réponse, veuillez agréer, Monsieur, l'expression de mes sentiments distingués.

Mlle Nathalie Aussans

(*Multilingual Business Handbook skeleton:* A15, O2, O3, O10, O11, O8, O25, E83, O34)

Bridgers Bank Ltd
King Street
Telford
Shropshire
England

22 July 19

Miss N. Aussans
12 Chemin des Abricotiers
La Tronche
38700 Corenc
France

Dear Miss Aussans

We thank you for your letter of 13 July and are pleased to hear that you wish to open a current and a deposit account with our bank. We can see no problem and have written to your Bank Manager, Mr Jourdan, for a reference. If this is satisfactory, the accounts will be opened upon receipt of the enclosed forms, which I would ask you to complete.

In answer to your questions, bank charges are payable only if your account is overdrawn. (We would allow you an overdraft limit of £100.00.) Bank transfers between England and France are subject to a short delay but rarely take longer than five days. Our branch has a cashpoint dispenser, which is open 24 hours a day, seven days a week.

A number of credit cards are available in Britain and we should be pleased to provide you with any further information you may require upon your arrival in Telford.

Yours sincerely

John Smith

Assistant Manager

(*Multilingual Business Handbook skeleton:* A5, A10, A19, O2, O3, I41, B65, G82, P8, O7, O18, E83, O16, O34, I107)

Continue the preceding exchange of correspondence by composing a third letter (in French) on the basis of the following notes.

To: John Smith (Bridgers Bank Ltd)

From: Nathalie Aussans

• Thank you for your letter of 22 July.

• Also for your further letter, confirming that accounts have been opened in my name.

• I wish to pay 1000 francs into my current account with you and have asked my bank to effect this transaction immediately.

• I shall be arriving in Telford next week and will call in to collect my cheque book and cheque card.

• Are there any British credit cards which can also be used in France?

• I look forward to meeting you etc.

Agexpo
124 rue du Château
77302 Fontainebleau
Tél: 60.64.40.00

Monsieur le Directeur
Sterlings Bank
Bridge Street
Coventry CV2 5TH
Angleterre

Fontainebleau, le 10 novembre 19

Monsieur,

Nos relations d'affaires avec vos clients Messrs. Watts & Grindley (Import-Export) ne cessent de devenir de plus en plus difficiles du fait que les virements bancaires de votre banque à la nôtre prennent de plus en plus de temps. Après vérification, notre banque a affirmé que ces retards provenaient d'outre-Manche.

Notre propre expérience nous fait croire qu'il en est ainsi. Par exemple, Mr Watts nous a fait savoir par téléphone, le 27 septembre, qu'il vous avait demandé de verser sur notre compte la somme de £1275.64. Cette somme avait été soigneusement calculée d'après le cours du change actuel. Nous avons alors donné à notre banque l'ordre d'émettre un effet bancaire irrévocable en faveur d'une tierce personne, après encaissement du virement, présumant que la transaction dudit virement aurait été faite en moins de 5 jours. La tierce personne nous a contactés le 12 octobre, nous priant de bien vouloir régler notre facture immédiatement, nous embarrassant ainsi considérablement. Nous avons reçu confirmation de notre banque qu'elle n'avait pas encore reçu le virement. De plus, votre banque, à qui nous avons téléphoné, nous a dit qu'il 'devait être resté en panne à un échelon quelconque du système'. Lorsque le virement est enfin parvenu à notre banque le 17 octobre, le montant était réduit de 282 francs à l'encaissement, par suite des fluctuations du marché des changes.

Le retard que vous avez mis à effectuer ce virement et d'autres opérations de change est tout à fait inacceptable et je compte recevoir vos explications par retour du courrier.

Veuillez agréer, Monsieur, mes salutations

G. Peyrefitte

Directeur

Copie: Banque Commerciale de Mâcon
          17 Place de la Gare
          77309 Fontainebleau
          France

(*Multilingual Business Database skeleton:* A76, E83, A27, E70, E71, E53, E84, E45, E42, E90, A53)

Sterlings Bank
Bridge Street
Coventry CV2 5TH

Tel: 0203 128 7354

22 November 19

For the attention of Mr G. Peyrefitte

Agexpo
124 rue du Château
77302 Fontainebleau
France

Dear Sir

We acknowledge receipt of your letter of the 10th inst, drawing our attention to the problems you have been having regarding bank transfers between your bank and ourselves.

We must point out straight away that international bank transfers are effected via a central computer in London, and that once the instruction leaves our computer terminal we have no control over how quickly it is transmitted abroad. Furthermore, I believe that the central computer was temporarily down from 30 September to 1 October, which probably accounts for the delay. This would explain why one of my colleagues said, in all good faith, that it 'must have got lost in the system'. The colleague in question has also informed me that the employee of your company with whom he spoke had a poor command of English and probably did not understand what was being said to him.

This type of transaction normally takes at most 5 days and hitherto our clients have been completely satisfied with our service. We regret you have found it necessary to complain about this matter, which was caused by factors beyond our control, and trust you will regard this as a satisfactory explanation.

Yours faithfully

John Smith
Manager

(Multilingual Business Handbook skeleton: A6, A1, A9, B27, E19, Q12, K70, D27, H6, F2)

Continue the preceding exchange of correspondence by composing a third letter (in French) on the basis of the following notes.

To: J. Smith (Sterlings Bank)

From: G. Peyrefitte (Agexpo)

- We acknowledge receipt of your letter of 22 November.

- Your 'explanation' came as some surprise to us.

- How can a 24-hour computer breakdown explain a 2 week delay in effecting the transaction?

- Why, in any case, was the transfer not made before the 30th, as it was authorised by Mr Watts on the 27th?

- The person who telephoned your Foreign Department was in fact English and understood only too well what was being said to him.

- Unless we receive payment of 282 francs within the next 10 days, we shall be forwarding copies of this correspondence to your Head Office in London.

SECTION 14: INSURANCE

This section is based on terms and expressions contained in Section P of the *MULTILINGUAL BUSINESS HANDBOOK*.

Assurances Métropolitaines
22 Boulevard Richard Lenoir
75011 PARIS

Tél: 49.78.30.61
Télex: 22445 ASSMET

Unicorn Insurance Company
51 High Street
Stratford-upon-Avon ST1 2LG
Angleterre

Paris, le 7 août 19

N/R: SB/Demande d'Indemnité No 42739/ET

Messieurs,

Une collision a eu lieu à Paris sur la chaussée du Boulevard Périphérique, direction est, à 19h20 le mardi 23 juillet, entre une berlinette Satra rouge, immatriculation 275 PIG 75, conduite par notre client M. E. Thibault, et une GT Mistral bleue, immatriculation D407 YOF, conduite par votre client Mr E. Blair.

Les deux conducteurs ont rempli et signé le formulaire européen de déclaration d'accident et M. Thibault nous a dûment fait parvenir sa copie. Selon la déclaration commune faite par les deux conducteurs, Mr Blair a changé de file afin de sortir du périphérique et prendre la direction Porte d'Orléans et M. Thibault, qui roulait lui aussi dans cette direction, a heurté l'arrière de son véhicule.

Nous croyons savoir que Mr Blair a une police d'assurance au tiers dont le numéro est V13/0274/114721/131 et qu'il possédait une carte verte lorsque l'accident a eu lieu.

Nous vous serions reconnaissants de bien vouloir nous confirmer que Mr Blair vous a signalé cet accident pour que nous puissions sans plus tarder fixer le partage des responsabilités et des frais de réparations à la satisfaction mutuelle des deux demandants.

Dans l'espoir d'une prompte réponse, je vous prie d'agréer, Messieurs, mes salutations distinguées.

Sabine Bardot
Service des Sinistres

(*Multilingual Business Handbook skeleton:* A14, P20, A2, P25, P28, P29, A123, P6)

Unicorn Insurance Company
51 High Street
Stratford-upon-Avon ST1 2LG

Tel: 0789 921 333

Your Ref: SB/Demande d'Indemnité No 42739/ET
Our Ref: SBDir5/AM1

14 August 19

For the attention of Mme S. Bardot

Assurances Métropolitaines
Claims Department
22 Boulevard Richard Lenoir
75011 Paris
FRANCE

Dear Madam

We acknowledge receipt of your letter of 7 August and can confirm that Mr Blair did report the accident to us, following his return from France on 24 July. We regret to inform you that there is a problem concerning his claim.

Whilst it is true that he was able to show M. Thibault a Green Card, the latter had unfortunately expired the previous day and was therefore no longer valid when the accident occurred.

This, plus the fact that the two drivers were unable to secure the names of witnesses, means that we are unable to accept either Mr Blair's claim or that of your client.

We hope that you will understand our position and deeply regret that we cannot accept liability in this case.

Yours faithfully

Simon Bernardes
Claims Department

(*Multilingual Business Handbook skeleton:* P6, A13, A6, A4, A9, P29, A31, P20, P28, F80, K32, P30, F83, A88, A43)

Continue the preceding exchange of correspondence by composing a third letter (in French) on the basis of the following notes.

To: Simon Bernardes (Unicorn Insurance)

From: Sabine Bardot (Assurances Métropolitaines)

- We are rather disappointed by your reply to our letter of 7 August.

- Our client risks losing his No Claims Bonus for an accident which was clearly not his fault.

- The accident occurred less than 24 hrs after the expiry of your client's Green Card, which must have resulted from an oversight on his part, and we would ask you to reconsider your position.

- Your client did, after all, have a valid third party policy.

- We think you have a moral duty towards our client.

Atelier des Arts Ménagers
14 Place Auguste Renoir
F-59049 LILLE

Tél: 20.55.47.06

Jackson Domestic Products
1035 Chamberlain Street
Slough SL7 5FY
Angleterre

Lille, le 12 septembre 19

Monsieur,

A la suite de notre lettre du 2 août et la correspondance qui en a résulté entre votre compagnie et nos assureurs, nous tenons à vous préciser le déroulement des événements tel que nous l'entendons.

1. L'expédition comprenant 2 caisses de 50 kilos chacune vous a été expédiée par camion le 15 juillet. La compagnie de transport en a pris la responsabilité et nous vous avons envoyé une copie du connaissement et également des documents d'expédition.

2. Ce chargement a été dédouané le 17 juillet par les douanes françaises et acheminé par vapeur Berlin. Il n'a pas été signalé, à ce stade du transport, que les marchandises avaient été avariées.

3. Le chargement est arrivé à Douvres le 18 juillet et a été entreposé dans un entrepôt de douane jusqu'au 22 juillet. Il a été dédouané le 22 juillet et est arrivé à votre usine le même jour. De même que les douanes françaises, les douanes britanniques n'ont signalé aucune marchandise avariée manifeste.

4. Cette expédition a été alors entreposée dans vos locaux le soir du 22 juillet et ouverte le lendemain matin. C'est à ce moment qu'on a remarqué que l'extérieur des caisses était cassé et qu'un certain nombre de machines à coudre étaient manquantes.

Notre assurance couvre normalement ce genre d'avarie, mais nous sommes certains que vous comprenez le point de vue de notre Compagnie d'Assurances. Tout indique que les caisses n'ont pas été endommagées en transit par une manipulation peu soigneuse, comme vous le prétendez, mais plutôt que les dommages et le chapardage se sont produits dans vos propres locaux.

Si vous ne pouvez faire preuve du contraire, les circonstances sont telles que notre Société et notre Compagnie d'Assurances se voient malheureusement dans l'obligation de refuser votre demande d'indemnité.

Je vous prie de croire, Monsieur, à l'expression de mes sentiments distingués.

B. Giroud
Service des Expéditions

(*Multilingual Business Handbook skeleton:* D36, D38, D51, D41, F62, E99, D60, D63, D126, D30, F33, D32, D135, E2, F17, F14, F63, F64, F19, F27, F59, D139, F33)

Jackson Domestic Products
1035 Chamberlain Street
Slough SL7 5FY
Bucks.

Tel: 0753 612 3772

19 September 19

For the attention of Mr B. Giroud

Atelier des Arts Ménagers
14 Place Auguste Renoir
F – 59049 LILLE
FRANCE

Dear Sir

We acknowledge receipt of your letter of 12 September. We must point out yet again that your insurance specifically covers goods damaged in transit by heat, by water, by rough handling and by pilferage.

We have done everything we can to help your insurance company to make further enquiries into this matter. We have provided them with an independent report listing the damage and the missing articles, contacted both the French and British customs authorities, and obtained a statement from the driver of the lorry. The Police have interviewed our warehouse staff and found nothing suspicious.

We do not believe that the damage occurred on our premises but that the goods were damaged in transit. We would like to point out that the fact that no damage to the goods was *reported* by the customs authorities does not necessarily mean that no damage had actually occurred. Customs officials cannot be expected to examine minutely all the goods which pass through their hands.

In conclusion we must insist on compensation for our losses and if we do not receive this by the beginning of next month we shall be forced to place the matter in the hands of our solicitors.

Yours faithfully

Robin Jackson

Director

(*Multilingual Business Handbook skeleton:* (A6, A1, A9, E19, F63, F27, F25, F26, F19, D139, F54, F82, F14, D130, J5, F27, E110, F33, F55, F56, E113, E121)

Continue the preceding exchange of correspondence by composing a third letter (in French) on the basis of the following notes.

To: Robin Jackson (Jackson Domestic Products)

From: B. Giroud (Atelier des Arts Ménagers)

- We have spoken to our insurance company once again.

- We have made clear your strong feelings on this matter.

- The insurance company is still not convinced that the damage occurred in transit, but is prepared to accept a compromise.

- It will reimburse up to 75% of the value of the damaged goods.

- We hope this will be acceptable to you.

- We apologise for all the inconvenience and bad feeling this incident has caused and hope we can resume our former happy trading relations.

SECTION 15: OFFICE TERMINOLOGY AND TECHNOLOGY

This section is based on terms and expressions contained in Section Q of the *MULTILINGUAL BUSINESS HANDBOOK*.

MANUDOC
10 route de Chantereine
78200 Mantes-la-Jolie

Tél: 14.77.11.66

MANUDOC (UK) Ltd.
41 Silicon Avenue
Basingstoke
Hants.
Angleterre

Mantes-la-Jolie, le 17 février 19

A l'attention de Mr J. Savage

Cher John

A la suite de ma discussion avec votre Directeur Technique, Mike Bowen, j'ai réfléchi
sérieusement au système informatisé que nous devrions choisir pour remplacer notre
système actuel. Il est dans l'intérêt de tous de standardiser le matériel utilisé dans toute la
Société, étant donné que la communication entre les différentes usines et également à
l'intérieur de chacune d'elles n'en serait que facilitée et les coûts réduits. Ce serait le cas en
particulier dans le contrôle des stocks et dans nos relations d'affaires avec les autres
entreprises.

C'est pourquoi je vous demande, à vous et aux directeurs de nos autres filiales, de me
procurer une liste de vos besoins en informatique et bureautique, en indiquant leur ordre de
priorité. J'espère ainsi pouvoir établir un consensus en ce qui concerne les besoins du
groupe dans son ensemble.

Jusqu'à présent, le seul avis prêtant à controverse que j'aie reçu provient de Mr Bruzzoni,
directeur de notre filiale italienne. Il pense que le télex devrait continuer à être séparé du
reste du système. Il semble que le télex ne cesse de se moderniser depuis 10 ans et Mr
Bruzzoni présente des arguments préconisant l'achat de nouveaux appareils hors ligne, qui
séparent la fonction préparation et la fonction émission; ces appareils autorisent la
mémorisation des messages et la réitération automatique des appels. Ils envoient également
des messages aux heures demi-tarif, supprimant donc le problème actuel des files d'attente
au télex.

Mon Directeur Technique a des vues totalement opposées. Il est d'avis que nous devrions
disposer d'un système informatisé complètement intégré grâce auquel chaque terminal
bureautique serait relié au réseau Télex national et international. Il affirme que de nombreux
systèmes sont équipés d'un automate qui gère l'émission des messages sur le réseau Télex.

.../...

De toute façon, au cours des 10 semaines qui suivent, j'ai l'intention de consulter les différents intéressés et dans l'attente de recevoir votre prompte réponse, je vous envoie mes meilleures amitiés.

Alain Faure

(Multilingual Business Database skeleton: A6, Q97, Q5, Q43, Q44, Q12, Q42)

MANUDOC (UK) Ltd.
41 Silicon Avenue
Basingstoke
Hants.

Tel: 0256 917 7272

8 March 19

Mr A Faure
Manudoc
10 Route de Chantereine
78200 Nantes-la-Jolie
France

Dear Alain

Thank you for your letter of 17 February.

As far as computer systems are concerned, I doubt whether our needs are any different from yours. Our Technical Director is in favour of purchasing a mini-computer which can drive up to 20 work stations. Ten of these work stations would be used mainly as word processors; at least one of them would also be used as a fax machine. The rest would be distributed among the various departments: Accounts, Personnel, Export, CAD/CAM, and Stock Control and Despatch. We would require the usual software packages and electronic mail facilities between the different terminals. We are also interested in expert systems for CAD/CAM.

Regarding Telex, we share Mr Bruzzoni's view, but for a different reason. If our entire communications system depended on a single processor and it broke down, we could no longer communicate with the outside world except by telephone. This would not be the case if we continued to have a separate Telex system, as Mr Bruzzoni suggests.

Hoping to have been of help to you,

Best Wishes

John Savage
Manager

(*Multilingual Business Handbook skeleton:* A10, A11, Q99, Q144, Q9, Q41, E27, I18, Q48, Q49, J11, Q71, Q38, Q52, Q5, Q42)

Continue the preceding exchange of correspondence by composing a third letter (in French) on the basis of the following notes.

To: John Savage (MANUDOC UK)

From: Alain Faure (MANUDOC)

- Thankyou for your letter and for the list of of your computer needs.

- Databases don't figure on the list, and I am assuming you will need appropriate software.

- How many printers will you require?

- Given the distribution of the machines in different departments, we think that 3 dot matrix, 5 laser printers and one plotter should be sufficient.

- I am considering your point about the separation of the Telex machine from the rest of the system.

- It does have some significant disadvantages, however.

Logi-Zen
1075 rue St.André
38002 GRENOBLE
Tél: 76 32 21 01

Infotek
2 Babbage Street
Reading
Berkshire
Angleterre

Grenoble, le 5 janvier 19

Monsieur,

Je vous remercie de votre demande de renseignements concernant notre EMUMIC 5000, actuellement le micro-ordinateur best-seller de vidéotex français. Je répondrai à vos questions dans l'ordre où vous les avez posées.

1. Il n'y a aucune contrainte technique qui empêche d'accéder d'Angleterre à Donétel, le système de vidéotex français.

2. La différence principale entre le Termitel et l'EMUMIC 5000 est la suivante. Le Termitel est un terminal dédié, c'est-à-dire qu'il est entièrement consacré aux applications offertes par le système Donétel et ne peut faire autre chose. Par contre, l'EMUMIC 5000, qui se raccorde au Termitel et utilise son clavier et son écran, revêt une double-fonction, étant en même temps terminal de vidéotex et micro-ordinateur, ce qui permet le stockage de l'information provenant du service Donétel consulté ainsi que le traitement local de cette information dans le cadre des fonctions informatiques classiques (traitement de textes, tableur, calcul). L'EMUMIC 5000 est donc un vrai micro-ordinateur qui autorise l'interface des fonctions vidéotex, bureautiques et informatiques, élargissant ainsi considérablement le champ d'action du Termitel.

3. Les coûts d'exploitation du système Donétel d'outre-Manche varient en fonction du moyen d'accès au système et du service consulté. Il y a 2 méthodes pour accéder à Donétel; la première utilise le réseau téléphonique ordinaire, en composant le 010 − 33, suivi du numéro d'accès au service Donétel et le code du service demandé; la seconde utilise le réseau britannique PSS (Packet Switch Stream) qui se relie à son équivalent français TRANSPAC (Transmission de données par paquets). La seconde méthode est nettement plus intéressante pour les usagers d'outre-Manche parce qu'elle évite de payer le coût d'une communication téléphonique internationale qui peut durer plusieurs minutes.

La deuxième variable dans le domaine des coûts d'exploitation est la nature précise du service consulté; certains services, tels l'annuaire électronique, sont gratuits, mais la majorité sont payants.

J'espère que j'ai pu fournir les renseignements dont vous aviez besoin et que vous n'hésiterez pas à vous adresser à moi pour tout renseignement complémentaire.

Félix Thierry
Service Technique

(*Multilingual Business Handbook skeleton:* A10, B21, Q7, Q32, Q12, Q138, Q10, Q8, Q9, Q56, Q36, Q146, Q35, Q145)

Infotek
2 Babbage Street
Reading Berkshire
England

Tel: 0734 511727

15 January 19

Mr Félix Thierry
Logi-Zen
1075 rue St. André
38002 Grenoble
France

Dear Mr Thierry

Thank you for your letter of 6 January. We are very interested in the EMUMIC 5000 and several of our customers have also expressed interest in the concept of linking a computer to a viewdata network.

You mention in your letter that the EMUMIC 5000 is connected to the Termitel itself. Does this mean that the Termitel's own modem provides the interface with the telecoms network, or must a modified modem be used? We would also like to know if the EMUMIC can be linked to the Telex network and, if so, whether it has an automatic call-back facility and can send messages at off-peak times.

Can you also let us know whether there is a list of Donétel services, containing the service codes to which you refer in your letter.

Yours sincerely

Hal Jones
Technical Director

(*Multilingual Business Handbook skeleton:* A10, A11, B6, B9, Q42, Q138, Q36, Q43, Q44)

Continue the preceding exchange of correspondence by composing a third letter (in French) on the basis of the following notes.

To: Hal Jones (Infotek)

From: Félix Thierry (Logi-Zen)

- Thank you for your letter of 15 January.

- The EMUMIC 5000 uses the Termitel's own modem and it can be linked to the Telex network.

- It can perform the functions to which you refer.

- A directory of Donétel services is available and can be obtained from the following address: 17 rue Pascal, 75001 Paris.

- It is updated every 6 months and the current edition lists over 2000 services.

- We would be interested in helping you launch the EMUMIC 5000 in the UK.

- I would be prepared to demonstrate the product on your premises.

- Please let me know if you are interested in this proposition.

APPENDIX: EXAMPLE CURRICULA VITAE & TESTIMONIALS

CURRICULUM VITAE

ETAT CIVIL

Nom: Prénom(s):

Sexe:

Date de Naissance: Lieu de Naissance:

Situation de Famille:

Domicile Permanent: Tél:

Domicile Temporaire: Tél:

Situation Militaire:

ETUDES SUPERIEURES

Etablissement(s):

Diplômes:

Matières:

STAGES:

LANGUES:

Séjours à l'Etranger:

EXPERIENCE PROFESSIONNELLE

Fonction Actuelle:

Emplois Occupés:

MOTIVATION:

LOISIRS:

REFERENCES:

CURRICULUM VITAE

ETAT CIVIL

Nom: REILLANE   Prénoms: Marie-France Jacqueline

Sexe: Féminin   Situation de famille: Célibataire

Née: le 18 mars 1964 à Ablon-sur-Seine (Val de Marne)

Domicile Permanent: 18 Avenue du Maréchal Foch,
                    94480 Ablon s/Seine   Tél: 45.97.66.42

Domicile Temporaire: 10 rue Grande
                     19120 Beaulieu s/Dordogne   Tél: 55.91.21.30

ETUDES SUPERIEURES

Etablissement: IUT Créteil

Diplômes: CAP dactylographie et sténographie – DUT

Matières: langage de base (techniques d'expression et de communication), mathématiques et statistiques, langues vivantes, dactylographie et sténographie, entreprise et environnement, informatique, problèmes juridiques, gestion commerciale, marketing, commerce international

STAGE: octobre/novembre 1985. Etablissements RODEX (St. Denis, Paris)

LANGUES: anglais – lu, écrit, parlé
         espagnol – lu, parlé

Séjours à l'étranger: Angleterre: assistante, Walsall School, 1985-6
                      Espagne: femme de chambre/serveuse, Hôtel de Madrid,
                               juillet-octobre 1986

EXPERIENCE PROFESSIONNELLE

Fonction Actuelle: adjointe à la secrétaire du Chef du Personnel, Compagnie des Assurances de Dordogne, janvier 1987...

MOTIVATION: Désire trouver un emploi utilisant anglais et espagnol. Accepte responsabilités, aime travail en équipe.

LOISIRS: lecture, musique, théâtre, randonnées, natation

REFERENCES: Docteur Gersant, 8 rue du Bac, 94480 Ablon s/Seine
            Mme Deniau, 21 rue Bridaine, 75017 Paris

CURRICULUM VITAE

Olivier LASSIGNY
41 rue Falguière
75015 PARIS
Tél: 42.86.55.63

Né le 12 septembre 1955
Marié – un enfant
Service Militaire: Exempté pour cause de double nationalité (anglo-française)

Diplômes

1973: Bac. Lettres
1976: Licence de Langues Etrangères Appliquées. Anglais. Université de Rhône-Alpes
1979: Maîtrise

Expérience Professionnelle

septembre 79 – mars 82: Porcelaines de Limoges – représentant outre-Manche

avril 82 -septembre 85: Rouen Optiques – Adjoint au Directeur des Exportations et du Marketing

septembre 85 à ce jour: Optic-Ingéniérie, Paris – Directeur Marketing

Stages

septembre 76-juillet 77: Assistant, Midland Institute of Technology

septembre 77-juillet 78: Lecteur, University of Stratford

septembre-novembre 1979: Stage de formation Techniques de Commercialisation, Porcelaines
de Limoges

Langues

Anglais: lu, parlé, écrit (niveau bilingue)
Allemand: lu, parlé, écrit
Russe: lu

Sports

Squash, tennis, ski, planche à voile

Etablissements Ceriel
22 route des Vosges
67054 Strasbourg

Strasbourg, le 5 mars 19

ATTESTATION

Je, soussigné, Thomas Darcy, Chef du Personnel des Etablissements Ceriel, suis heureux de transmettre les observations suivantes sur Monsieur VILLEBOIS Yves.

Monsieur Villebois a été nommé au poste d'adjoint au Directeur du Marketing en avril 1985. Il devait aider à créer et gérer une équipe de marketing qui aurait comme responsabilité de rechercher et identifier les créneaux dans le marché de nos produits, puis de décider comment combler ces créneaux. Il était également chargé de réorganiser notre service de ventes.

Cette dernière tâche, que Monsieur Villebois a assumée entièrement seul, n'a pas été aisée mais Monsieur Villebois s'en est acquitté avec tout le tact et la fermeté qu'elle demandait. Il s'est avéré très consciencieux, organisé, capable de prendre rapidement des décisions mais soumettant néanmoins un travail minutieusement étudié. En fait, Monsieur Villebois excelle là où il est entièrement responsable de la conduite d'une étude, plus que dans un travail en équipe où sa forte personnalité, son enthousiasme, son esprit innovateur et sa vive intelligence l'empêchent parfois de se mettre à la portée de personnes moins douées que lui.

Nous regrettons de ne pouvoir jouir plus longtemps de la collaboration de Monsieur Villebois avec lequel nous avons eu d'excellentes relations. Mais nous comprenons fort bien qu'une personne ayant l'ambition de réussir tienne à avoir une expérience des affaires dans différents domaines. Nous espérons qu'il réussira dans cette nouvelle entreprise.

Université de Rhône-Alpes II
Domaine Universitaire
BP 46 X – 38010 GENEPI
Tél: 76.77.92.66

SECTION DE LANGUES ETRANGERES APPLIQUEES

Génépi, le 6 septembre 19

ATTESTATION

Mlle DORIOT Clémentine

Je, soussigné, Pierre Klemperer, Directeur de la Section Langues Etrangères Appliquées de L'Université Rhône-Alpes certifie que Mlle Doriot a été employée comme dactylographe au secrétariat de notre Section pendant l'été de 19..

Elle a fait preuve d'application et d'exactitude dans son travail qui nous a donné toute satisfaction. Elle a participé à toutes les activités de secrétaire de notre département de façon très intelligente, faisant preuve d'initiative dans l'utilisation des différents appareils qui lui ont été confiés et a rapidement maîtrisé les problèmes auxquels elle a dû faire face.

Nous ne pouvons que complimenter Mademoiselle Doriot sur son travail et sur son comportement qui lui ont acquis de nombreux amis dans notre section.

LinguaWrite

Automatic multilingual business letters

What is LinguaWrite?

LinguaWrite is an exciting and versatile software package for creating business letters in the *five* major European languages. LinguaWrite is the ideal software companion for the *Multilingual Business Handbook* and *Multilingual Business Correspondence Course*. It is specially developed for use in business and education.

What can I do with LinguaWrite?

Using LinguaWrite you can:

- have access to the *Multilingual Business Handbook* database of 2000 specialised phrases in each language: English, French, German, Italian and Spanish
- put these phrases into your word-processor without needing to type them
- search the complete database for key words or multiple key words or limit this search to a particular section
- browse through the database, as if leafing through the book, and select the required phrase at the press of a key
- enter the alphanumeric code given in the book and have the translation instantly
- with just a few keystrokes, build up business letters, like building blocks, instantly on screen
- change the source and target languages at will
- change the menus and messages into any of the five languages at a touch of a key.

The program caters for accents and special non-English characters and these appear correctly in your word-processor as long as it can support the full character set. (An additional package is available to customise national keyboards that do not support the full range of European characters.)

Simple to use

The program is very simple to operate and you can begin work in a few minutes. The accompanying manual is clear and straightforward and written for those who are unfamiliar with computer technology as well as for more expert users.

LinguaWrite is available for BBC and IBM (and compatible) computers.

For more information and prices, please contact:

MultiLingua
FREEPOST
LONDON W4 3BR
Tel.: 01-995-0478